THY ROD
and
THY STAFF

They Comfort Me

Christians and the
Spanking[1] Controversy

SAMUEL MARTIN

---

[1] Please note that through out this version of the book the word "smacking" is used. This term is identical in English to the term "spanking" which is more commonly used in the USA while the term "smacking" is used in countries associated with the British Commonwealth.

This volume is dedicated to my parents, Dr. Ernest L. Martin (1932-2002) and Helen R. Martin. Thank you for your love and for your desire for me to be a part of your family.

First Edition - Winter 2006

Samuel Martin
Email: info@biblechild.com

Recompense to no man evil for evil. Provide things honest in the sight of all men. If it be possible, as much as lieth in you, live peaceably with all men.

Dearly beloved, avenge not yourselves, but rather give place unto wrath: for it is written, Vengeance is mine; I will repay, saith the Lord.

Therefore if thine enemy hunger, feed him; if he thirst, give him drink: for in so doing thou shalt heap coals of fire on his head.

Be not overcome of evil, but overcome evil with good.

Romans 12:17-21

TABLE OF CONTENTS

Introduction 9
"Thy Rod And Thy Staff They Comfort Me"

Chapter 1 15
The phases of child development outlined in the Bible
The Biblical data defining what is a child
A definition of terms

Chapter 2 33
Jewish attitudes toward the texts advocating smacking in the book of Proverbs
Jewish opinions about the Proverbs speaking about smacking
Jewish attitudes toward strictness in general
Before a smacking…
Instruments of smacking
Does the rod always mean a stick?
The age for smacking
Understanding the orientation of Jewish scholars to their religious texts

Chapter 3 50
The legal context of the book of Proverbs
The legal orientation of King Solomon and King Hezekiah
So how do we understand the Book of Proverbs today?

Chapter 4 59
The gender focus of the book of Proverbs
The Book of Proverbs: A background
Context is important
Wisdom literature
The Biblical collection devoted to feminine themes
The masculine context and tone of the book of Proverbs
Application to concept of smacking
Smacking only for the male sex?
The book of Proverbs and its masculine orientation
Doesn't the Bible mean both sexes when it refers here to the male gender?

Chapter 5 76
The New Testament and the texts advocating smacking in the book of
Proverbs

Chapter 6 83
The New Testament references to physical punishment
Jesus and the act of driving out the Moneychangers

Chapter 7 88
Will a smacking save your child from going to Hell?
The use of "sh'ol" in the Bible
The modern beginning of the problem: The King James Version

Chapter 8 98
"Chasten thy son while there is hope, and let not thy soul spare for his crying"
The use of the word "*crying*" in the book of Proverbs

Chapter 9 104
A rod is for the back or the buttocks?

Chapter 10 108
The Theological Interpretation of a smacking

Appendix 1 115
Misunderstanding the harshness in Biblical Teachings

Appendix 2 121
Punishment: Does it work? A Biblical Examination

Appendix 3 129
The Biblical uses of the word "*Sh'ol*" and the variances in English Translation
found in the King James Version

Appendix 4 133
The Biblical uses of the word "*Shevet*" and the variances in English Translation
found in the King James Version

Appendix 5 140
The order of the Hebrew Bible books versus the order found in Protestant
Bible versions

Appendix 6 143
St. Augustine on corporal punishment

INTRODUCTION

Thy Rod and Thy Staff They Comfort Me

There are few subjects that cause passions to stir among people more than that of smacking children. This issue cuts right to the heart of questions concerning parental rights, correct methods of child rearing, appropriate punishment, freedom to raise one's children as one chooses and a host of other issues.

This issue pits two main groups one against the other. On one side of the issue there are those who take the religious position that smacking is beneficial for children because it is a teaching found in the Bible. Those who espouse this position have their proponents among pastors, Bible teachers, ministers, lay people in the church, religiously motivated psychologists and even among politicians who are either affiliated with religious movements or who believe in the necessity of smacking children. On the other side of the issue there are those in the human rights community, particularly focusing on children's rights, secular psychologists, doctors, university professors, and social workers.

Numerous non-profit organizations have been formed to advocate for and against this practice and hundreds of thousands of Pounds are spent to promote the idea and to discredit it. Debates that take place on television or radio are some of the most rancorous exchanges and studies are analysed, quoted, referred to, reinterpreted, discredited or agreed with. Some religious proponents even point out to their adherents that this practice is so fundamental to freedom of choice for parents to raise their children the way they wish under the religious system of their choice, that if children's rights proponents have their way, parents will be prosecuted and thrown in jail for giving their children a swat on the bottom. Certainly, this kind of information stirs people up into action. So much so that attempts to pass legislation on the part of politicians are stifled over and over again by their desire not to offend their religious constituents. However, does all of this need to be?

My experience with this subject

I was raised in a very strict religious home and when I did things wrong, smacking was the chosen method of "correction." One of my earliest recollections as a small boy was being spanked in Interlachen, Switzerland for getting too close to the edge of a mountain guardrail. I, like so many people before me, was taught that these smackings were good things to help me become a better person. I believed this teaching to be the truth of God. However, in 1996 that all changed for me.

In 1996, I began to do some research work into my favourite book of the Bible: the book of Proverbs. Most of the work was simple word studies and reading commentaries about the book in general. It did not take me long to develop an interest in smacking children. At that time, I began to think about how I would raise my own children. Would I spank them like I was spanked myself? Initially my answer to this question was "yes."

That all changed when I read a book by Dr. Philip Greven titled: "*Spare the Child: The Religious Roots of Punishment and the Psychological Impact of Physical Abuse.*" This volume opened up the whole issue of smacking for me in a different way than I had ever looked at it before. Probably the most important thing I learned was that there were conservative Christian leaders who themselves had been spanked as children, but they chose to adopt a new method for raising their children. The Reverend Dwight Moody was such a man as Dr. Greven points out.

Rev. Moody was a giant of evangelical Christian work in the last half of the nineteenth century. His conservative approach to the Bible is without question, yet he chose not to spank his children! He chose to adopt grace, not law, as the ruling principle in his home. This to me was a revelation in knowledge.

As soon as I came upon Dr. Greven's work, I began to read other books such as *"For Your Own Good"* by Alice Miller. I can remember hearing Dr. John Bradshaw refer to this volume as I have followed his work since the early 1990's. I found this new book interesting and valuable, but I was also during this time really looking closely at the Biblical information regarding the whole matter of smacking.

What I began to see what that there were major problems with many of the ideas being promoted among those in the religious community surrounding this issue. I also found that the disagreements that many in the children's rights community were voicing were simply based upon what those in the religious community were advocating.

I began to see that what was taking place was based upon incorrect information being presented about what the Bible says about smacking children. I then began to think that this work might necessitate a full-length book on this subject.

My findings

The first thing I discovered is that most religious proponents of smacking children have not seriously researched the Biblical texts that they use to support this teaching. Most proponents of smacking have many supporters in the religious community. Most people simply quote a few passages in the book of Proverbs as their authority and think there is little else needed to do.

This is problematic especially concerning the question of what the Bible says about children. Most religious teachers do not point out that the Bible, in the original Hebrew language in particular, (which the bulk of the Old Testament and the book of Proverbs were originally written in) uses more than nine different words in Hebrew to describe the various phases of life for children up to adulthood. This was a revelation to me because all of the verses in the book of Proverbs focus on a single word translated as children, but not referring to young child under the age of about ten!

I also learned that numerous sources from the Jewish world exist that offer a fascinating glimpse into their understanding of this subject and how they interpret these verses. In this regard, I came across a book written in 1989 by Meir Munk titled: "*Sparing the Rod: A Torah Perspective on Reward and Punishment in Education.*" This volume opened my eyes to the wealth of knowledge available from Hebrew sources about this subject which Christians rarely quote or refer to.

I also analysed all of the texts from the book of Proverbs that are found in the New Testament. Not once does any text most often quoted by smacking proponents[2] advocating smacking children ever appear in the New Testament. It seemed reasonable that if the early Christian writers of the Bible advocated smacking children, they would simply have quoted from the book of Proverbs from one of these texts, which seems to point to smacking children and use that as their authority for suggesting the practice, but not one of them did.

I also saw the importance of understanding the book of Proverbs in its legal context. Without this knowledge, one will find interpreting the whole book correctly difficult. The legal context of the book of Proverbs affects all the information in it and I found out that the writers of that book all had a legal orientation towards the Biblical books of Moses[3] and the legislation outlined therein. There is nothing wrong with the system outlined by Moses. However, Christians are not under the Law of Moses, we are under the Law of Jesus Christ.[4]

I also learned that it is important to understand the gender focus of the book of Proverbs to interpret the information in it. I came to see that the

---

[2] Proverbs 10:13, 13:23,24; 19:18; 22:15 & 23:13,14
[3] The first five books of the Bible, which are Genesis, Exodus, Leviticus, Numbers and Deuteronomy.
[4] John 1:14

whole book is not designed for or oriented toward the feminine gender at all. The whole book is masculine in tone, substance and advice and today the information in that book is still designed mainly for men.[5]

I also learned that there are major translation problems affecting two of the verses that smacking advocates most often point to as their primary evidence for smacking children. One verse is used by many religious proponents of this practice to teach parents that if they don't spank their children, they risk sending them to eternal Hell fire. Another verse points to the need to bring tears when giving a smacking. The only problem with both of these verses is that they are both based upon faulty translations from Hebrew and this has been demonstrated clearly with the modern scholarship available in the last one hundred years.

I also learned that the idea of smacking children on the buttocks is an interpretation offered by many smacking proponents with no real support in the Biblical texts at all. This teaching has developed from religious teachers with no real authority from the Holy Scriptures.

I also saw that theologically speaking the whole idea of a smacking is not congruent with the teaching revealed in the gospel of Jesus Christ. God sent His Son into the world to save the world so they would not have to suffer for their own sins, but parents today punish their children and make them undergo the horrors of punishment for even the most minor of infractions. The idea of mercy is seemingly not applied at all. When parents sin, they ask God to forgive them, repent and know they are forgiven. When children sin, they are judged, tried, condemned, and punished.

I also learned that those in the children's rights community need to take care how they interpret the Bible. Many of the anti-smacking advocates attack the Bible on the basis of taking a verse here or there out of context.

---

[5] Certainly, there is practical advice that women can use, but the textual orientation of the whole book is decidedly towards men.

This is dangerous and should not be done. Biblical interpretation should be left into the hands of those who are trained to do so.

The rest of this volume documents all of these findings listed above. I have presented these findings in the hope it will help people to understand and possibly change their minds as I have.

The goal of this book is to help show Christians who love the Bible and non-Christian critics of the Bible that there is a middle ground where we can meet and discuss issues that are important to our children, families and our culture.

It is my hope that in some small way I have met this goal with the publication of this work.

Samuel Martin
Jerusalem, Israel

1

The phases of child development outlined in the Bible

There is a commercial that appears regularly on Israeli television and it features a beautiful house being demolished. The workers are there with a crane and a huge wrecking ball is demolishing a house. The owner of the house then enters the picture with a look on her face of absolute disbelief. The workers then take the work order showing the house number to be "68." They then turn the work order over and find out that the house number should have been "89." This was a simple mistake with catastrophic consequences.

This commercial illustrates one of the biggest problems today facing advocates of smacking. This is because virtually all advocates of smacking simply say that the Biblical teachings regarding smacking relate to "*children*" without any elaboration or definition grounded in solid Biblical information. So what constitutes a "*child*" from the Biblical point of view? Just who is being discussed in the texts in the book of Proverbs? Scores of pastors, Bible teachers and even authors of authoritative Bible commentaries are quick to point to the texts in the book of Proverbs as their primary evidence in favour of smacking, but few seem to bother with seriously examining the data in question. This seems to represent a fundamental error. It is exactly the same as the Israeli commercial. What Christian parents must do is to examine these texts carefully to make sure they are speaking about "68" instead of "89."

It is not appropriate to simply quote the five texts in Proverbs that refer to the "*rod*" as the authoritative evidence for smacking children and imagine that there is little else to discuss in this matter. This does a disservice to the book of Proverbs itself, the whole of the rest of the Bible, and especially the New Testament.

In this chapter, we are going to carefully look at the information that the Bible provides us as well as what it does not provide us. Both are equally important. By doing this, it is hoped that instead of looking at the number "68," we actually are referring to the number "89."

The Biblical data defining what is a child

What is a child? When does one begin being a child? When does one stop being a child? How does the Bible look at this question? These questions need to be asked and answered when it comes to even the most rudimentary of understandings about smacking children. We simply need to know how the ancient people of the Bible looked at the concept of childhood.

How did the people mentioned in the Bible look at their children? What defined a child in their world? What were the various phases of childhood as outlined in the Bible and how can we understand them? These questions are extremely important to ask and to answer. This is because we need to accurately interpret to *whom* the Biblical texts in the book of Proverbs suggesting smacking are directed.

To embark upon a study of the matter of the development of children in ancient Jewish society, one must first examine what Jewish people have said about children in their own works. This makes sense because it is the Hebrew Bible (the Christian Old Testament) that contains the texts that virtually everyone advocating smacking refers to. In opening this investigation, it is amazing what is available for the researcher, but it equally more surprising what is not available. It is very surprising that more has not been written on the development and environment of children in the Bible, but it appears that up until now few have been asking the questions that are now being posed by those interested in the history of child development in ancient cultures.[6]

There are a number of interesting Jewish sources written by Rabbis, some of whom are ancient and other of which are more modern. However, these volumes are not a part of the mainstream body of reference literature available to Christians for several reasons. First, there is a lack of connection between Christian and Jewish scholarship and there are also language barriers. Many of their ancient volumes are written in Hebrew, Arabic, Yiddish, Aramaic or other languages and are simply not available to those outside of the traditional circles of Hebrew and Semitic scholarship. There are few ways for people, not knowledgeable of Jewish writings and without the needed language skills, to access the wisdom of these giants of Biblical scholarship.

From a more academic viewpoint, we also don't have a lot of books on the subject of Jewish attitudes toward children. In a recent book on the Jewish family, David Kraemer, who authored the section of this volume concerning "*Images of Childhood and Adolescence in Talmudic Literature*," says the following: "When asking about that other species of children (here the author is speaking of information concerning childhood development that would interest the professional student of childhood issues), we have woefully little to work with."[7]

Additionally, Kraemer points out that he was only able to find one book solely devoted to the subject of speaking "of the traditional attitude toward Jewish children."[8] This book, "*The Jewish Child*," by W.M. Feldman, as Kraemer points out, found so little information about Jewish attitudes toward children that Kraemer said: "Feldman was forced to pad the book with chapters on such matters as mathematics in the Talmud, presumably

---

[6] See Kramer, The Jewish Family, pg. 64-66, 1996.
[7] Kraemer, The Jewish Family, pg. 66
[8] ibid.

because children learned math in school."[9] Kraemer provides a great deal of excellent information from the period in which the Talmud was written (from the third century BCE until the fifth century CE), but as for a treatment of the child in the Bible itself, there is very little information available from Jewish sources.

Solomon Schecter, the English Hebrew scholar who was active in the last part of the last century published a short article about children in a Hebrew journal, but his article was a basic introduction to children's themes in the environment of Jewish history. Certainly, this article is interesting and valuable, but it does not focus on a detailed analysis of the book of Proverbs or any of the texts relating to smacking.[10]

However, some excellent Jewish sources are available. One of the most illuminating volumes in English (for those interested in the Jewish perspective on education and child rearing and texts related to child rearing in the Bible) is the book titled "*Sparing the Rod: A Torah Perspective on Reward and Punishment in Education.*"[11] This volume reveals several important sources of the abovementioned Jewish works. This volume is an amazing glimpse into the wisdom of Jewish learning.[12] This book refers to many works written by Rabbis, but most of these works are not available currently in English translation. This is why this volume is so valuable because it gives us a glimpse into the depths of Hebrew scholarship.

Now if some Jewish scholars, who do not have the New Testament as their Holy Scripture, are pointing out that the Biblical, post-Biblical and historical sources are vague concerning specific information about children

---

[9] ibid., pg.66-67

[10] Solomon Schecter, Journal of Jewish Studies

[11] Author is Meir Munk, Mishor Publishing Co. Ltd., Bnei Brak, Israel 1989. For more information about this volume contact Judaica Express in the USA at 1800 2 BOOKS 1.

[12] I wish to thank Rabbi Reuben Feinstein, the son of the late eminent Rabbinical scholar, Rabbi Moses Feinstein of New York, for his permission to quote this book. I highly recommend it to anyone interested in the Jewish perspective on this issue to get a copy of this volume mentioned in this paragraph.

and how ancient Hebrew society looked at them, how is that Christian ministers or Bible teachers can come along now and explain what the texts of the Hebrew Bible mean relative to children when individuals whose expertise far outstrips those of us in the Christian world are saying that they don't have the answers to these questions? This is one question that those in the Christian world who advocate smacking children need to answer.

Thankfully, some important work has been done in this regard by the eminent Christian Hebrew scholar, Alfred Edersheim. He was a Christian scholar who was intimately familiar with all of the Hebrew body of scholarship and his knowledge of Jewish religious sources was first rate.

A definition of terms

A good place to begin any discussion is with a definition of terms. In the Hebrew Bible (the Old Testament), there are quite a number of terms that are used to describe children at various phases of life. Edersheim in his invaluable work "*Sketches of Jewish Life*" says the following: "The tenderness of the bond which united Jewish parents to their children appears even in the multiplicity and pictorialness of the expressions by which the various stages of child-life are designated in the Hebrew [in the Hebrew language]. Besides such general words as '*ben*' and '*bath*' [these are Hebrew terms and their meanings follow here] -- 'son' and 'daughter' -- we find no fewer than nine different terms, each depicting a fresh stage of life."[13] These phrases "*ben*" (Hebrew: son) and "*bath*" (Hebrew: daughter) are used hundreds of times in the Bible and are general terms used to describe, sons, daughters, children and a person's age.[14]

---

[13] Edersheim, Sketches of Jewish Life, pg. 103

[14] In Hebrew, when asking someone's age, even today in the modern language, you say: "The son (or daughter) of how many years are you?" This may seem an odd way to ask this question to the English ear, but this is how it was done in ancient times and this is also how it is done today.

This is an extremely important statement. What Edersheim is saying is that the phrases in Hebrew that describe children and childhood are distinct and are also characterized by an almost visual element. This will become more evident when we look at the examples given by Edersheim, but this point cannot be mentioned without some commentary. There is a reason for this. When we look at terms in the Bible that describe actions directed at a certain person or group, because we are dealing with a very old text that is culturally disconnected from our modern world by many hundreds of years, we need to be sure that the group in our modern world that we are applying these texts to are the same group in the ancient world that the people at that time applied the same information to. If we don't do this, then we can misapply the information we are looking at by applying it to a group of individuals for whom it was never intended.

This is where the main problem comes in understanding to *whom* the texts in the book of Proverbs were directed. If we assume that they were just applied to "children" in general without any definition, we run the risk of misapplying the text to a subgroup of the category of "children" who were never intended to be the recipients of such teachings. This is where great care is required in knowing and correctly applying the Biblical information that we do have. This approach seems to be a sensible one. It seems that we really don't have another choice in this regard because apart from direct commentaries from the writers themselves, how can we be absolutely certain that what we are saying about a text represents the meaning that the author intended? First, we have to clearly define the terms we are discussing. Then we can consider to who these terms are to be applied. We then have to look at how these terms are used throughout the Bible to determine God's definition of them. This is the best course of action to take to understand whom we are talking about. It is also very important to carefully consider the information that we do have and not dismiss something as unimportant. The entire Bible is important and valuable.

What we find in the Hebrew Bible is that, just as we have in English, we have terms that very specifically describe the various phases of childhood. By understanding these terms and by correctly applying them to the Biblical texts that refer to them (and not applying them to the Biblical texts that don't!), we position ourselves on a more equal level when it comes to comparing who is being discussed in one section and who we can apply those teaching to today. Let us look at these various phases now.

When we are willing to take a fresh new look at childhood in the Bible, we can see, as did Alfred Edersheim, that the words employed by the Biblical writers are very visual in nature in describing the various stages of child development. Edersheim opens his examination of this important matter with the following: "the first of these [terms designating phases of child development] simply designates the babe as the newly 'born' -- the *'yeled'* or, in the feminine, *'yaldah'* -- as in Exodus 2:3; 2:6; 2:8. [these texts in Exodus concern the baby Moses]"[15]

It is important here to mention what Edersheim meant by his use of the word "pictorialness" in describing the words used to point to the various phases of child development in the Hebrew Bible. The way that these words convey a visual or "picture like" sense is by connecting them to the Hebrew verbs from which the nouns are constructed. In Hebrew, the word *"yeled"* (masculine) or *"yaldah"* (feminine) are both related to the verb *"yalad."* This verb simply means, "to give birth."[16] So the meaning of the noun of the same root refers to the one who came from the giving of birth. This is the "pictorialness" that Edersheim refers to. This verb, in various forms is found several hundred times in the Bible.[17] This word is given a very clear meaning as referring to the time in the life of a child from birth to the time of weaning. Look at the following verse from the book of Genesis that shows this very

---

[15] ibid., pg.104
[16] See Genesis 4:18; 4:22; 6:4; 10:8
[17] Wigram's Englishman's Hebrew and Chaldee Concordance (WEHCC), pg. 527-530

clearly. "And the child (Hebrew: *yeled*) grew, and was weaned."[18] [Historical sources show that this weaning took place at the age of three.[19] More on this later.]

We also find a logical approach to naming various stages of children's lives in the Bible. This takes place through specifying names based upon actions taking place in the lives of the children themselves. By understanding that the use of certain words relates to actions that children specifically are doing (that point to a time in life that they are doing them), this will help us to correctly understand what stage of life is being referred to in the Biblical verses related to children.[20] Rather than just referring solely to "children," we can better define the time in the life of these "children" and by doing this we can begin to put flesh on the skeletons that are these Biblical texts. Let us now return to Edersheim's discussion with these points in mind. They will help us to understand the words that are used in the Bible to describe these important phases in the life of children.

To demonstrate the subtle difference a word can bring Edersheim says the following: "But the use of this term [the term refers to the word *'yeled'* which means 'babe'] throws fresh light on the meaning of some passages of Scripture. Thus we remember that it is applied to our Lord in the

---

[18] Genesis 21:8

[19] Mc'lintock & Strongs: Cyclopedia of Biblical, Theological & Ecclesiastical Literature, vol. II, pg. 243, article. *'child,'* which refers to Genesis 21:8; Exodus 2:7,9; I Samuel 1:22-24; II Chronicles 31:16 and Matthew 21:16

[20] This concept is not strange to the English language either. For example, look at the verb "drive." This word refers to an action of moving something from one place to another. It can refer to something such as a "driving a car or a tractor," but it can also refer to things such as animals, like "driving a herd of sheep." Now, what is the noun form of this verb? It is driver. So, the noun and the verb form of a word are closely connected in English as well as Hebrew. Hebrew only is different in the sense that each word has its own gender while in English gender is express through the use of adjectives or pronouns. In English, we say "a male driver or a female driver." In Hebrew, there is no such use of these helping words because each word has its own gender. So, to say "male driver," in Hebrew it is only one word "*nahag.*" Female driver is "*nahagah.*" (Hebrew in this sense is similar to Spanish, which incorporates the gender into the word directly such as "senor" (gentleman), or "*senoritah.*" (lady)

prophecy of His birth:[21] 'For a babe (Hebrew: *yeled*) is born unto us, a son (Hebrew: *ben*) is given to us.'"[22] This word *"yeled"* appears almost 90 times in the Bible.[23]

Edersheim continues: "The next child-name in point of time, is *'yonek,'* which means, literally, 'a suckling.'"[24] Note that Edersheim specifically uses the phrase "in point of time." This is because each of these names follows the other as far as time is concerned. This word in Hebrew comes from the verb *"yanak"* which literally means, "to suck."[25] In English, we would refer to these children as "infants" or "nursing babies."

In fact, there are two different terms in the Bible that describe two different periods of a suckling child. The first term *"yonek"* refers to babies who are in the period of life that is characterized as receiving nourishment only from their mother's breast. These are children who are aged from birth to about 12 months or so. After 12 months or so, children begin to eat other food other than that provided by their mothers through nursing, but they are also still nursing. This takes place, depending upon what culture you are referring to, anywhere from 12 months until a child is about two and a half or even three.

This transition from receiving nourishment through suckling only to a combination of suckling and eating solid food is mentioned in the Bible by referring to a different term to point out this new phase. (In the Bible, the age of three was the time for weaning officially as mentioned previously.) The term that describes this phase of life of suckling as well as eating some solid food is the Hebrew word *"olel."* "As the word implies, the *"olel"* is still 'sucking;' but it is no longer satisfied with only this nourishment, and is 'asking bread,' as in Lamentations 4:4: 'The tongue of the suckling child

---

[21] Isaiah 9:6

[22] Edersheim, Sketches of Jewish Life, pg. 104

[23] See WEHCC, pg. 530

[24] Edersheim, Sketches of Jewish Life, pg.104

[25] This verb appears 32 times in the Hebrew Bible and in every occasion refers to sucking, suckling or nursing. See WEHCC, pg.542.

(*yonek)* cleaves to the roof of his mouth for thirst; the newly eating children (*'olelim'* - plural of the word *olel*) ask bread."[26] (translation mine) Edersheim continues: "This word, *'olel,'* refers to a child who is not weaned yet but still periodically nurses at its mother's breast.[27]

One point that must be made regarding these two terms is that they are distinct and refer to two specific phases of life. An "*olel*" is always older than a "*yonek.*" The point that differentiates these children is the fact that some are eating food from their mothers only, while others are supplementing their mother's milk with food from other sources.

Note the following quotes that show this: "Out of the mouth of babes [28] and sucklings[29] hast thou founded strength because of thy enemies;"[30] Note also: "to cut off from you man and woman, child[31] and suckling[32]…"[33] This is ample evidence to demonstrate the distinction in these terms. The term "*yonek*" (or its related words) is found 32 times in the Bible[34] whereas the term "*olel*" occurs 20 times.[35]

Logically, the time following the period of a child nursing at the breast is characterized by a specific term in Hebrew just as it is in English. This is the fourth designation found in the Bible. It "represents the child as the *'gamul'* or 'weaned one,'"[36] from a verb which primarily means to complete, and secondarily to wean."[37] This verb, which jointly means "to complete" and "to wean," shows the child completing the nursing phase. There are several texts in the Bible that specifically refer to this completion

---

[26] Edersheim, Sketches of Jewish Life, pg.104
[27] ibid.
[28] Hebrew - *olelim* – plural of *olel*
[29] Hebrew – *yonekim* – plural of *yonek*
[30] Psalm 8:3
[31] Hebrew - *olel*
[32] Hebrew - *yonek*
[33] Jeremiah 44:7
[34] WEHCC, pg. 542
[35] WEHCC, pg. 907
[36] Psalm 81:2; Isaiah 11:8; 28:9
[37] Edersheim, Sketches of Jewish Life, pg.104

of the weaning phase. They refer to a variety of situations and personalities. For example, it is mentioned in the book of Genesis "that Isaac was weaned."[38]

King David also spoke about humility and pursuing a life of peace and tranquillity. He compared this to a weaned child sitting next to his mother. In this comparison, he shows that he had come to learn to humbly approach life and not to seek things that were beyond him. In doing this, he became aware of an inner peace and found a sense of completeness. This feeling he compares to that of weaned children who find that when they complete the nursing process, they find a sense of peace and quietness resting beside their mothers. This is an extremely beautiful and deeply sensitive comparison from the inspired pen of King David[39] who refers to this weaned child as sitting next to his mother.[40] We find that the phase of life for these children is between the ages of three to four. Note again that a *"gamul"* is always older than an *"olel."*

This period is followed by another term mentioned by Edersheim. These years are times of particular closeness to their mothers, even clinging to her. He described it like this: "After that the fond eye of the Hebrew parent seems to watch the child as it is clinging to its mother -- as it were ranging itself by her -- whence the fifth designation, *'taph.*[41] The use of this word is further defined when we look at some of the verbs that are related to this noun. We find that the reason that Edersheim referred to this term as showing a child "clinging to its mother" or "ranging itself by her" is because the verbal uses of this noun refer to the English word "swaddled." This term refers to the ancient custom of women wearing swaddling bands. These were exterior garments that were band-like in construction and were a

---

[38] Genesis 21:8
[39] Psalm 131
[40] ibid.
[41] Edersheim, Sketches of Jewish Life, pg. 104; See also Esther 3:13, The *'taph'* and the women in one day; Jeremiah 40:7; Ezekiel 9:6

handbreadths or so thick and were used to carry children by their mothers. This verb is used in a beautiful description of God's right hand "spanning" the heavens.[42] This word "spanned" means swaddled. It shows that God cares for the heavens in the same way that a mother with child cares for it and brings it close to her with her right hand. We even find that the earth in ancient times had a "swaddling band" around it.[43] This was a circular band like ring similar to that found around other planets.[44]

We also have the Bible referring to "swaddling clothes" which were garments that were used on very young children who were yet to be trained in normal bodily functions. These garments were used to wrap the child around their body and could easily be removed quickly to facilitate a child who needed to relieve him or herself. These garments were wrapped close to the body in a circular fashion.[45]

In using this word "*taph*" it gives the strong impression that Hebrew mothers were intensely close to their children and their children stayed very close to their mothers throughout the time prior to the age of six years. This idea is beautifully taught in an extremely touching verse found in the book of Isaiah that describes the birth of a whole nation in one day who will be "carried upon her sides, and be dandled upon her knees. As one whom his mother comforts, so will I comfort you."[46] This is just more evidence that women in ancient times carried their young children and swaddling bands were a part of this process.

In closing this discussion about the word "*taph*," we find this phrase used 42 times in the Hebrew Bible and it universally refers to "little

---

[42] Isaiah 48:13

[43] This "swaddling-band" was disturbed in the time of Noah and caused the Flood according to research conducted by Dr. Ernest L. Martin, my father and an extraordinary interdisciplinary Christian scholar. See his booklet "Solving the Riddle of Noah's Flood" (ASK Publications:1987)

[44] Job 38:9

[45] See Luke 2:7 and 2:12

[46] Isaiah 66:12-13

children."[47] This period refers to young children who are between the ages of four to six years. After age six, then began a process of either continued closeness to the mother for girls or separation from the mother for boys and beginning a new life spending most of their time with their fathers.

Continuing, Edersheim says: "The sixth period is marked by the word '*elem*' (in the feminine, '*almah*,' as in Isaiah 7:14, of the virgin mother, which denotes becoming firm and strong."[48] This is time in life mentioned in the Bible is when a young person is approaching adolescence. This word is translated in English by words such as "maid," "damsel," "virgin," "stripling," and refers to those young people who are not yet even young adults. These words are today called "pre-teenagers" in modern language. These words together are found nine times in the Bible.[49]

Now, as we have in English there is another term that refers to the time just after and including the teenage years, where the young person is now starting to gain some sense of independence. Edersheim phrases it this way: "As one might expect, we have next the '*na'ar*,' or youth -- literally, he who shakes off, or shakes himself free.[50] [The word *na'arah* is the feminine form of this word *na'ar* and it is also found frequently in the Bible.[51]] This word is found over 200 times in the Bible.[52] There are some poetical uses of this phrase "*na'ar*,"[53] but the vast majority of these texts refer to younger men or women who have yet to marry.

---

[47] WEHCC, pg. 484

[48] Edersheim, Sketches of Jewish Life, pg. 104

[49] WEHCC, pg. 943

[50] Edersheim, Sketches of Jewish Life, pg.104

[51] Genesis 24:14; 34:12

[52] WEHCC, pg. 823-4

[53] In the book of First Samuel, Chapter 1, we find the word "*na'ar*" being used of Samuel immediately following his weaning in v.24. It is used several times also in Chapter 2 during the stage of Samuel growing up. It is clear that Samuel was brought to live in the Temple when he was a very young boy. It is also clear that from where he lived in Ramah, the Temple was at that time in Shilo, less than half a day's journey away. While he was away from his mother, he had plenty of supervision living in the Temple at that time. The reason for the use of this phrase

One term that Edersheim does not refer to in his treatment of this issue is the word "*bthulah*"[54] We find this word used to refer to the phase of life for young women just immediately prior to marriage. Girls in this stage of life were referred to by the phrase "*bthulah*." This word means a young woman who has not participated in sexual intercourse, or specifically, a *virgin*. This is the exact meaning and there are numerous texts to show this.[55] This word appears 50 times in the Bible.[56]

Edersheim, concludes his discussion of these terms with the following: "Lastly, we find the child designated as '*bachur*,' [the feminine is *bachurah* but this word is apparently not found in the Bible] or the 'ripened one;' a young warrior, as in Isaiah 31:8; Jeremiah 18:21; 15:8."[57] Note again, Edersheim uses the word "lastly" which shows a continuing time element in discussing the terms. This phrase is where we start to see words describing marriage being coupled with those describing this phase of life. Note the following: "For as a young man (*bachur*) takes to himself (in marriage) a virgin (*bthulah*), so shall thy sons take thee to themselves, and as the bridegroom rejoices over the bride, so shall thy God rejoice over thee."[58] So we find that the phrase "*bachur*" refers to a time in the life of young men, where marriage starts to become a reality. Men in the Biblical and post-Biblical periods generally married between 13 and 17 and women generally married between 12 and 18.[59]

---

to describe him in this stage is not clear, however, he was "shaken free" from his home life at an early age to prepare him for the great tasks he underwent.

We see the same phrase used of Moses who was only a small baby at the time in Exodus 2. This phrase is coupled with the previously mentioned term "*yeled*." It seems clear from the context that Pharaoh's daughter was speaking poetically. The dialogue almost sounds like a mother saying: "Look here at this little man crying!"

[54] Which in English means "*virgin*."
[55] Note Deuteronomy 22 in particular
[56] WEHCC, pg. 284
[57] Edersheim, Sketches of Jewish Life, pg. 105
[58] Isaiah 62:5
[59] Mc'lintock & Strong's: Cyclopedia of Biblical, Theological & Ecclesiastical Literature, vol. V, pg. 775.

Finally, the last two words that describe the final stage of life, adulthood, are man and woman. In Hebrew, these terms are for man, *"ish,"* and for woman, *"ishah."* These terms are only mentioned here for continuity and reference, as we are not specifically discussing them in this context. They appear hundreds of times in the Bible.[60]

Edersheim concludes his comments regarding these terms by saying the following: "Assuredly, those who so keenly watched child-life as to give a pictorial designation to each advancing stage of its existence, must have been fondly attached to their children."[61] Of this there is no question. It is quite interesting that the ancient Hebrews had specific designations for each phase of human development, much like our modern English terms newborn, infant, nursing child, toddler, preschooler, prepubescent, pre-teen, teenager, young adult and adult.

What the evidence from the Bible shows is that the Biblical writers had specific terms that they employed to each phase of life. The catchall phrase "child" is not sufficient to describe the multiplicity of terms used by the Biblical writers.

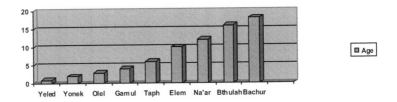

Conclusion

Now that we have defined and placed these terms in context, let us now consider how to better understand the Biblical passages that refer to these

---

[60] WEHCC, *"ish,"* pgs.60-69 (over 1,600 times); *ishah*, pgs.175-178 (over 550 times)
[61] Edersheim, Sketches of Jewish Life, pg. 105

terms. At the very beginning of the book of Proverbs we have an introduction that orients the reader to the book as a whole. This section mentions that the book is directed to the "young man."[62] This word for "young man" (Hebrew: *na'ar*), as the previous analysis has shown, does not include young men who fall into the pre-teen category. Let us look at the evidence that shows this.

As mentioned earlier, the Hebrew terms that refer to the phases of life are "*yeled*," "*yonek*," "*olel*," "*gamul*," "*taph*," *elem*," "*na'ar*," "*bthulah*," "*bachur*," "*ish*" and "*ben*." Let us now look at the occurrences of these terms in the book of Proverbs.

Now, the words "*yeled*," "*yonek*," "*olel*," "*taph*," "*bthulah*," are peculiar in the book of Proverbs for one important reason. This is because they are not found once in any verse in the whole book in either masculine or feminine forms. Additionally, the words "*bachur*," "*gamul*," and "*elem*" are found only once.[63] The most prominent of these listed words found in the book of Proverbs is the word "*ish*" which means "man." This word also overwhelmingly refers to grown men. This word is used in the book of Proverbs 84 times.[64]

The word that we find used in three of the verses that advocate smacking in Proverbs is "*na'ar*."[65] The phase of life associated with the "*na'ar*" (which means the "one shook lose") is that of young adulthood or the teenage years. This is significant. Based on this evidence, it is safe to say that all of these texts in the book of Proverbs have no application to anyone less than about ten to twelve years of age.

---

[62] This suggestion has been reiterated by Dr. Randall Heskett in Interpretation Journal April 2001 article: "Proverbs 23:13-14," pgs. 181-4. This is an article by a professor with expertise in Old Testament Hebrew.
[63] For *bachur,* see Proverbs 20:29 and for *elem,* which in this case we find the word in the feminine gender being "*almah*" see Proverbs 30:19. For *gamul,* the verbal form *gamal* is found in Proverbs 11:17, but in this case, the context does not refer to a child being weaned.
[64] WEHCC, pg.67-8
[65] Proverbs 22:15; 23:13-14; 29:15

The other two verses[66] often quoted by smacking advocates when referring specifically to the recipient of the corporal punishment both refer to the word "son." In Hebrew, the word used is "*ben.*" This word is used hundreds of times in the Bible and can refer to a son of any age. In light of the use of this word, "son," it makes sense, considering especially that we have three others texts that all refer to the use of the "rod," that we let these three texts, which use the Hebrew word "*na'ar,*" be our primary sources of authority to understand who was the recipient of such corporal punishment.

Obviously, we cannot let the two texts, which use the word "son" (Hebrew: *na'ar*) let us interpret the three texts, which use the more specific term "young adult" or "teenager." All who are fathers refer to their teenage boys as their "sons," but not all fathers' sons are teenagers. We have to let the more precise term young adult or teenager, which in Hebrew is "*na'ar,*" be our guide when applying these texts to individuals.

In conclusion, this evidence shows that the book of Proverbs is referring to a specific phase in the life of a person. It is not referring to "children" in the non-specific way.

We have to be very careful in handling the information that we do have from this book because this information is sparse and terse. We also need to be very careful not to read things into the texts that are not there on the basis of an English translation. We have to let the original Hebrew words and their meanings come through into our understandings or else we can lose the richness of meaning that is there for the interested party to investigate.

This advice must be especially heeded when it comes to such issues of immense social importance as how we bring up the next generation. For their sakes, we need to be right and protect them from teachings that are not directed at them in the first place.

With this information in mind, let us now look at some further evidence concerning early and modern Hebrew conceptions about smacking

---

[66] Proverbs 13:23,24 and Proverbs 19:18

and the book of Proverbs. It will pay great dividends to pay attention to the words of some of the great Hebrew scholars who devoted their lives to Bible study.

2

Jewish attitudes toward the texts advocating smacking in the book of Proverbs

It is amazing that there is a very little contact between Jewish and Christian scholars regarding the subject of smacking. [This is really unfortunate. We Christians can learn a lot about the Bible from our Jewish brethren.] When you look at Orthodox Jewish works regarding child rearing, you will not find any references at all concerning Christians or Christianity. This is almost the same among more liberal Jewish writers. And why not? Most Jewish writers are writing for Jewish audiences. The same is the case for Christians. Most are writing for their own constituencies, so there is actually very little contact on scholarly levels, certainly in this subject area. This is unfortunate, but understandable.

From the earliest of my recollections, I was brought up in an environment of deep respect for all Jewish scholarship regarding the Hebrew Bible (the Old Testament). This started for me at a very early age. I lived in Israel for almost one year of my life prior to the age of seven. In addition, I can always remember my dad having a huge collection of religious books to conduct his work as a Christian theologian. He always had a great respect for and constantly referred to an innumerable number of Jewish books and Jewish religious sources. [My father held his library in very high esteem and he had particular reverence for his books devoted to Jewish scholarship.]

This is because of two reasons. First, the Hebrew Bible is written in Hebrew and Aramaic and the best people to understand it are those who are trained in those languages. Second, these books represents the history of the Jewish people, so it will pay us great dividends to be aware of and respect the opinions of the scholars who have devoted their lives to the study of and bringing of clarity to the religious texts that they hold with such holiness, purity, esteem and respect.

Jewish Opinions about the Proverbs speaking about smacking

How have Jewish scholars understood the texts in the Book of Proverbs that advocate the use of the rod? Let us consider this question. By understanding the Jewish point of view in regard to these texts, this will help us to see how their scholars have looked at these texts over the centuries.

At this point, let us refer to an invaluable volume mentioned previously. It is an English translation of a book that originally appeared in Hebrew in 1989. It is titled: *"Sparing the Rod: A Torah Perspective on Reward and Punishment in Education"* by Mr. Meir Munk.[67] This volume was produced under the direct approbation of and spiritual guidance of the eminent Israeli Torah sage and contemporary Rabbinic scholar, Rabbi Samuel HaLevi Wosner of Bnei Brak, Israel.

Jewish attitudes toward strictness in general

Before going into the question about Jewish attitudes toward smacking, it must be pointed out that strict religious observance is something that is demanded of adherents to the Jewish faith. However, there are right and

---

[67] Sparing the Rod: A Torah Perspective on Reward and Punishment in Education by Meir Munk (Bnei Brak: 1989) To get a copy of this excellent book call Judaica Express at 1800 2BOOKS1. It is with great appreciation that I acknowledge the fine work of Mr. Munk, the publishers, Mishor Publishing Co., Ltd., of Bnei Brak, Israel and Rabbi Reuben Feinstein of Brooklyn, New York (the director of Mishor Publishing Co. Ltd.). Rabbi Feinstein is the son of the eminent Torah scholar Rabbi Moses Feinstein of Brooklyn, New York. He graciously granted his permission for this volume to be quoted here. I strongly recommend this volume to any parent or teacher who wishes to dig in deeper to the immense wisdom and depth of knowledge available from the pen of Jewish scholars surrounding this subject

wrong ways to go about creating a sense of strictness among religious adherents. Mr. Meir Munk summarizes the opinions of Jewish scholars surrounding their attitude towards children in the following six rules:

"A. Strictness gives rise to resistance, and is therefore negative.

B. Instead of being strict with a child, we should get him to want to be strict with himself.

C. Since we are not thoroughly familiar with the powers of the psyche, we may do damage by being strict. Strictness is best minimized, or done away with altogether.

D. Study should lead to the *yiras shamayim* (Hebrew: a respect for heaven) and service of God. The teacher[68] must convey the sanctity and the affection which produces *yiras shamayim*.

E. Quiet, patient explanation is the only way to teach.

F. The 'Rod of Pleasantness' is to be preferred to the 'Rod of Severity.'"[69]

Following up on these thoughts, one of the well-known sages of the Talmud, Abba Eliyahu commented also on this idea of strictness. "The Torah (the Bible) is understood only by people who are not strict. I, too, reveal myself only to people who are not strict by nature."[70]

The point to these texts is clear. An environment of life for children that is too strict is not conducive not only to learning secular information, but also for a healthy, mature spiritual development that leads to a strong and lasting faith. For religiously inclined parents, the last thing they wish is for the actions that they are taking for their children's perceived benefit to actually be counterproductive. In this regard, strictness, in all forms, according to rabbinical authorities, is to be strenuously avoided.

---

[68] I think that Mr. Munk would agree that adding the parent here makes sense as well.
[69] Munk, pgs.31-32.
[70] ibid. pg. 156.

Before a smacking…

In the circles of Jewish scholarship, we find a large body of information about events that should take place prior to a smacking. This is because a smacking is not the place to start with eliminating bad habits or traits. If used at all, it is the last resort. A good example of this is found in the statement by Rabbi S. N. Brazovsky who confirmed this by mentioning the following: "To attempt to stamp out [bad traits] with ill will and corporal punishment is like dousing a fire with oil. Instead, we must hold our temper and show the child an even greater amount of boundless love and mercy than we had previously."[71]

Smackings are punishment. They are given in response to acts that take place. No one in their right mind would take their youngster aside and say: "Look Mary, you are a really great kid and there is no reason to spank you specifically, but I am going to give you a smacking anyway to remind you that you are supposed to behave well." Obviously, such a suggestion is crazy. Jewish scholars will have no such part of the previous suggestion. They take this matter of punishment very seriously and it can only take place under certain circumstances. We must understand that there is a whole system of events that can and should take place prior to a smacking ever being considered. Let us also understand that while many of the suggestions we find in Jewish sources refer to the child and his interaction with the school and the authorities associated with schools, many of the principles pointed out apply also to the home and the training taking place therein.

The first thing that must be understood is that "punishment and reproach are necessary. But like most good things, punishment is most useful and beneficial when it is rare. The less frequently it is imposed, the more effective it will be."[72] Before punishment can take place, three preconditions must be in place. These are: a warning has taken place; never punish out of anger, and make absolutely 100% certain that the child deserves the

---

[71] ibid., pg. 54.
[72] ibid., pg. 63

punishment. Without all of these items being in place, you can in no way attempt to effectively administer punishment.

Types of punishment

While the work of Mr. Meir Munk focuses on events taking place in a school environment, it is quite easy to relate these examples given below to the home environment. The first is a comment about a particular event. Next, if a comment is not effective, a warning should be given. After a warning, comes the threat. (In this regard, children should never be threatened with punishment at a later time because of a key legal case in which a parent threatened his child with a beating at a later time and the child went and committed suicide. This legal event in Jewish legal history has profoundly affected all interpretations surrounding smacking since the time when this event took place over 1700 years ago.)[73]

After a threat, a reprimand should be employed. If these techniques do not work, Jewish sources recommend writing the child's name in a book designed to document instances of misbehaviour.[74] Should these not prove effective still, a punitive writing assignment is suggested.[75] After that, belongings could be confiscated. Should this still not prove effective, removal from class celebrations could be considered. Obviously, removing a child from the learning experience is to be avoided as the entire previously mentioned points take place in the classroom environment. Ejecting a student from class is a very serious matter and should only be undertaking on serious reflection. This could also take place for a few minutes, not the whole class period. Sending a child to the principal is also a serious matter that should be avoided and used sparingly. Only after these points have been

---

[73] Masekhes Semachos Chapter 2.

[74] This technique is found in the Bible in the Old and New Testament. Writing someone's name in a book is characterized as a very serious event. See Exodus 32:32 and Revelation 3:5 and 13:8.

[75] In this regard, Jewish scholars strongly recommend against a writing assignment that could create a feeling of dislike for the Bible. See Munk, pg. 75.

exhausted is smacking considered in a classroom setting. This is because smacking represents the most serious of approaches to punishment. All other avenues of punishment should first be tried before resorting to this method.[76]

Because the relationship of a parent and teacher are somewhat similar when it comes to the question of punishment, we can see here in this summary that there are many things that parents can also do, according to Jewish scholarship, prior to even thinking about the need for a smacking. These include many listed in the previous summary, but one could also include sitting quietly for a few minutes, asking a child to go to their room, not making a favourite food dish or many such similar things that could be used in an escalating way. There are, of course, dozens of excellent books that one could get which could suggest a hundred things or more one could do to punish your children without ever having to think about a smacking first.

Instruments of smacking

The first and probably most interesting aspect of Jewish interpretation surrounding the verses concerning smacking is the instrument used to conduct the smacking itself. Now the Biblical teaching in the book of Proverbs seems quite clear. The only item mentioned six times without ambiguity is the rod.[77] Now, how have Jewish scholars applied these texts in Proverbs when it comes to the instrument for punishment? First, note one of the earliest sources which refers to this subject mentions that "shoe straps" or "shoe latchets" are the chosen instrument to administer a smacking.[78] Confirming this idea we have several Rabbi's agreeing with this statement. Rabbenu[79] Gershom said: "Hit [the child] with a shoe strap, but not too

---

[76] Munk, "Sparing the Rod," pgs. 63-102. Please refer to the text for too many references to quote here.
[77] Proverbs 10:13, 13:24; 22:15; 23:13; 23:14 & 29:15 where the Hebrew word *shehvet* is used for rod.
[78] Babylonian Talmud, Tractate Baba Bathra 21A.
[79] Rabbenu means "our Rabbi" from the Hebrew language.

much, because excessive beating will not make him wise."[80] This statement seems to be completely contradictory to all of the teachings referring to the wisdom found in the "rod" mentioned in Proverbs. Rabbi Solomon Ben Isaac[81] also "specifies 'shoes latchets' (shoe straps); that is, a light blow which can cause no injury."[82] The learned Hebrew Christian scholar Alfred Edersheim mentioned the same idea. Speaking about a classroom setting he said: "The teacher was to endeavour to secure the confidence, the respect and the affection, both of parents and children. The latter he was to treat rather with kindness than with rigor. Beating, if necessary, with a strap,[83] *never with a rod*, was to be the principal means of correction;"[84] When you consider the statements about the rod from the book of Proverbs it is almost inconceivable that Edersheim could write such a statement, but he did!

One of the more illuminating quotes concerning this matter gives a good outline of the approaches found in Jewish schools when discipline was necessary. "Discipline was to be maintained, but punishment should be mild. For physical chastisement a light strap only was to be used. Persistent insubordination was not to be visited with expulsion; the offender was rather to be subjected to the salutary influence of his more tractable schoolfellows. Leniency was preferred to rough measures."[85] We also find the monumental work, *The Shulchan Arukh*, referring to the preferred instrument for smacking: "Teachers must not administer beatings (a) like cruel enemies, (b) with a whip, or (c) *with a rod*. Instead, a little strap should be used."[86] Once again here we see the rod forbidden, not encouraged, as the means to administer a smacking.

---

[80] Munk, Sparing the Rod: A Torah Perspective on Reward and Punishment in Education, pg. 86.

[81] Known in Jewish circles by the acronym RASHI.

[82] Munk, Sparing the Rod, pg. 86.

[83] Referring here again to Babylonian Talmud, see above note 3.

[84] Alfred Edersheim, History of the Jewish Nation (Grand Rapids: Baker Book House) 1954, pg. 278.

[85] Hastings, Encyclopedia of Religion and Ethics, art. *Education (Jewish)*, p.195.

[86] Shulchan Aruch, Yoreh Deah 245:10, quoted in Sparing the Rod, pg. 86.

In summary, excessive discipline was avoided, the use of the rod was forbidden, suspensions or expulsions from school were frowned upon and to enhance the behaviour and learning ability of a sub-standard student, it was suggested to get him a tutor who was one his own age.

The late Torah scholar Rabbi Moses Feinstein also echoes this previous suggestion. He said: "In my humble opinion, I think a teacher should not strike a pupil even lightly with a stick or anything that may cause severe pain when wielded with force. A teacher should not use such an instrument to frighten pupils. Thus, he should not clutch a stick at all, but rather keep a little strap handy.[87]

Rabbi Feinstein goes even farther regarding the use of a stick specifically when it comes to children. He commented on another opinion offered by two other Rabbi's saying: "You did well by quoting the late Rabbi Reuben Grazovsky, who cited Rabbi Shneur Zalman (Shulchan Arukh HaRav) to the effect that one who hits another with a stick is in violation of the commandment against injuring a fellow Jew. It appears that even if he dealt him a gentle blow with the stick – *since he may not strike a child with a stick at all* – it is tantamount to having struck any Jew. In this case, he has violated the commandment even with a gentle blow which causes no injury.[88] The violated commandment under discussion by Rabbi Feinstein is found in Exodus 21:18.[89]

Other suggested instruments of smacking are suggested from Jewish sources. Several authorities mention the hand. Rabbi Moshe Auerbach "suggested that one strike a child only with one's hands, because then the discipliner, too, feels the pain; when the pain increases, he will stop."[90] This

---

[87] Munk, Sparing the Rod, pg. 122.

[88] ibid., pg. 123.

[89] What this section of the book of Exodus shows is that it is against the law for one person to injure another by fighting or similar activities.

[90] Munk, Sparing the Rod, pg. 87.

statement, on the surface, seems to be directly contrary to Proverbs 19:18.[91] Rabbi Yisrael Meir HaCohen Kagan, known in learned Jewish circles as the Chofetz Chaim, also chose to use his hands to punish, not straps or rods. His son, Rabbi Arye Leib mentions the following: "When I was little and was naughty – especially when I insulted someone – [my father] would slap me in the face. Because a slap in the face is meant more to embarrass than to cause pain, a very slight slap was enough. Bear in mind, then, that one slaps a child on the face to embarrass, never to cause pain."[92]

Finally, we have also have the following anecdote about one who used a ruler to administer corporal punishment. This short anecdote points to the prevailing attitude that Jewish scholars in general hold about those who attempt to inculcate wisdom into children by the means of force. "It is reported that a certain young teacher used to discipline pupils by striking their fingertips with the edge of his ruler ... until he slipped and struck his own hand. He never used that tactic again."[93]

What the data show are that even though there is an undeniable focus on the use of the rod as the sole instrument of punishment mentioned in the book of Proverbs, some of the greatest minds of Jewish scholarship have suggested other instruments and some have even religiously ruled against the use of the rod even though it is mentioned in the Bible. These Jewish scholars opinions today also happen to be binding and authoritative in understanding the Bible. The Bible actually cannot be interpreted in Jewish circles without the opinion and approbation of authorized rabbinical authorities.

Does the rod always mean a stick?

One of the more interesting things about Jewish scholars is their approach to this question. In actual fact, we find that several rabbinical authorities have

---

[91] See Chapter "Chasten thy son while there is hope, and let not thy soul spare for his crying."
[92] Munk, Sparing the Rod, pg. 87.
[93] ibid.

found broader meanings to the verses in Proverbs advocating smacking. One of the most interesting is from Rabbi Shlomo Wolbe. Speaking about education and the classroom environment, he said: "'Speak…calmly,' the Talmud[94] tells us, 'for then your words will be heeded.'[95] Rabbi Wolbe explains that 'this is the great rule…in education. Anything said differently will [generally] go unheeded. The only way to educate is calmly and patiently. After all, that which is axiomatic to the teacher is new to the pupil.

The latter is, in a certain sense, being asked to reconstruct his character. Even when a child does not immediately do as told, the educator should not punish him at once but rather alert him to his duties with quiet firmness. When punishment does become necessary, bear in mind that the rod King Solomon speaks of ('He who spares his rod hates his son…[96]) is to be understood in a broad sense. It includes many things, such as a frown and pretended disappointment. As implied by the word '*musar*' at the end of the verse, the true discipline is the kind that which touches the youngster's heart. The tender heart of a child is greatly upset when a parent [or anyone from whom he expects appreciation] expresses any measure of distress at his behaviour.

The prophet [Zecharia] can help us to understand the concept of 'rod' more deeply. He says: "…I took for myself two rods [staffs]: one I named Pleasantness and the other Severity…"[97] It emerges that there is [not just one 'rod' for disciplining – even when understood broadly, as above. There is] a rod of pleasantness as well, and one can use it even more successfully than the rod of severity…' What is the 'rod of pleasantness' in education? Keep the following rule in mind: 'Encouragement makes a greater

---

[94] The Talmud is the central document containing Jewish legal opinions beginning about 200 BC and continuing until about 500 AD.
[95] Babylonian Talmud Tractate Shabbat 34A
[96] Proverbs 13:23-34
[97] Zechariah 11:7

impact than punishment; praise and reward go farther than threats or penalties.'"[98]

Rabbi Wolbe reminds us of another passage that bears mentioning in this regard. This is from that most familiar of English sections of the Bible. "The Lord is my shepherd; I shall not want. He makes me to lie down in green pastures: he leads me beside the still waters. He restores my soul; he leads me in the paths of righteousness for his name's sake. Even though I walk through the valley of the shadow of death, I will fear no evil: for thou art with me; **thy rod and thy staff they comfort me**.[99]

King David, who wrote this passage, found in the rod a sense of pleasantness as Rabbi Wolbe pointed out. Obviously, in this passage, there is no thought of the rod being a punishing instrument at all.

The age for smacking

One of the important aspects of corporal punishment concerns the age when a smacking should take place. The Bible uses the word *"na'ar"*(youth) to describe those to whom smackings are to be directed.[100] What do Jewish scholars say about this point? The information that we do have is sparse, but we do have an opinion concerning students. According to this source, children under age 6 should never be spanked at all: "It emerges from the entire discussion[101] here in the Talmud, according to the *Maharsha*,[102] that this only applies from the age of six – and only after a gentle verbal appeal has failed. A child under six, however, is not hit even lightly for refusing to learn. The teacher tries to reach him through gentle speech."[103] This train of

---

[98] Munk, Sparing the Rod, pg. 31

[99] Psalm 23:1-4

[100] See chapter "The phases of child development in the Bible" in this volume for the data that demonstrates this.

[101] The discussion referred to here took place between 2 rabbis. It is from the Babylonian Talmud, Baba Bathra 21A.

[102] This phrase *"Maharsha"* refers to an authoritative commentary written on these Talmudic texts at a later time.

[103] Munk, Sparing the Rod, pg. 90.

thought relates well with the Biblical evidence related to the Hebrew words used to describe pre-adults.[104]

Children under age six were not ready for education outside of the home. A Rabbinical scholar points out that "if you set your child to regular study before it is six years old, you shall always have to run after, and yet never get hold of it."[105] This thought is further clarified with the following statement. In the article *Parent and Child* under the sub-heading, 'Different Rules for Boys and Girls' in the prestigious Encyclopaedia Judaica, we read the following: "halakhic scholars[106] laid down that children below the age of six years must be in the custody of their mother, since at this tender age they are mainly in need of physical care and attention. Above the age of six, boys must be with their father, since at this age they are in need of education and religious instruction, a task imposed by law upon the father, and girls with their mothers ('the daughter must always be with her mother'), since they are in need of her instruction in the ways of modesty."[107]

Other rabbinical authorities point out the reason for this. They noted that young children simply couldn't understand intellectually why they are being punished and what punishment is meant to do for them. Their intellectual capacity has not been developed. Note the following: "A young child – too young to understand why he is being punished – is sitting next to his father who is studying religious books. [Suddenly, the father notices that] the little one is about to relieve himself. He should not rebuke him. The child simply will not understand that the books are the cause of the rebuke [not his need to relieve himself], and he will respond by restraining himself out of fear – thereby endangering himself…"[108]

We can see from early records that Jewish scholars were very sensitive to the need to handle small children carefully. Upon entering school

---

[104] See chapter "The phases of child development in the Bible" in this volume.
[105] Babylonian Talmud, Tractate Ketuvot 50
[106] Halakhic scholars refer to scholars of Jewish legal principles.
[107] Encyclopedia Judaica, vol. 8, pg.98.
[108] Munk, Sparing the Rod, pg. 85-86.

at age six children were sheltered from subjects that might be discouraging to the young mind. Subjects dealing with sin and atonement, the afterlife and judgment were strenuously avoided.[109] These subjects require a more mature mind and this idea is absolutely reflected in the teachings of Jewish scholars.[110]

A clear theme running throughout religious Jewish thought (that relates specifically to the matter at hand) is outlined in the following: "Discipline is most effective in the age of puberty. Therefore forbearance is recommended with pupils until the age of twelve, but strictness after that, because youths from that age onward begin to show mental capacity and acumen."[111] We can see that it was strongly felt from the earliest of times that children who were too young did not understand physical punishment, so for them it was not used. Those over the age of 13 were legal adults[112] in many respects and they were expected to adhere to the religious rules outlined in the Jewish faith. As pointed out earlier, this information relates well to the use of the word "na'ar" in Proverbs describing those best suited for the use of physical punishment in that period.

In closing, we can see the evidence points to the fact that young children were not the objects of either the texts of the book of Proverbs or the interpretations of those texts by later Rabbinical authorities. With this in mind, we today should also take these facts into account when interpreting these texts.

---

[109] Edersheim, Sketches of Jewish Life, pg.135-136.
[110] For more information in this regard, see Cohen's, Everyman's Talmud, pgs. 173-180.
[111] The Jewish Encyclopedia, art. *Pedagogics*, p.572
[112] See chapter "The Phases of Child Development outlined in the Bible"

Understanding the orientation of
Jewish scholars to their religious texts

To complete this discussion, one thing must be mentioned. Jewish scholarship does allow for smacking, or corporal punishment. It is, however, permitted only under the strictest of circumstances. It is not being suggested that this is not a fact. It is a fact, but it is very important to understand the ways in which Jewish scholars arrive at binding Biblical interpretations to this day. These interpretations are arrived at with the greatest of deliberation and care and are not haphazardly formulated.

In closing this chapter, the following should be pointed out concerning Jewish interpretations of this or any subject related to their faith. These discussions can only take place under certain circumstances and involving recognized religious authorities. Without the input of a recognized Rabbinical authority, conclusions concerning religious matters cannot be arrived at. This may seem strange on the surface to those outside of the Jewish faith, but this is an absolute fact that affects every aspect of the life of the religious Jew.

When one objectively thinks about it, it is quite logical to have religious guidance and beliefs being formulated by recognized authorities. These recognized authorities are Rabbis who make up the various bodies of Judaism. While you do have several divisions in the Jewish community, all of the adherents to these various groups recognize the divinely inspired authority that has been placed in the rabbinical bodies that interpret Jewish Law.

One of the 613 commandments required of the religious Jew is to recognize and submit to the authority of a recognized body of Rabbis. This commandment is as follows: "According to the Law which they shall teach you, and according to the judgment which they tell you, shall you do; you shall not turn aside from the sentence which they shall declare unto you, to the right hand nor to the left."[113] This concept has been known and accepted throughout the period of Judaism's history. The reason for this is clear.

Note the following: "The question arises concerning one who desires to be selective in his submission to Jewish law. The Torah, in this *mitzvah* (commandment), admonishes us that we may not be discriminatory in our obedience to Jewish law; whatever the Rabbis teach as *Halakah*[114] must be accepted. If this principle were abandoned, the result would be a number of legal systems in Judaism, each pandering to the whims and follies of people, each of whom would select the law that best suited him. This is obviously impossible in a strong, purposeful and orientated society such as the Jewish community."[115]

What this quote shows is the rationale for how Rabbis are allowed to interpret their religious and historical texts for today and create binding rules that are in force. If people do not adhere to the new rules, they are breaking the previously mentioned commandment that gives the authority to do this to the Rabbis. This idea is further reinforced by the earliest of Jewish scholars. They said: "If we believe in the authority of Moses, it follows that we must also believe in the authority of the succeeding sages. To deny the entire tradition of rabbinic influence on Jewish law or to stultify it by not acknowledging its continuity is tantamount to abrogating the entire legal system. In other words, either we believe that contemporary rabbinic authority is as binding as was that of Moses and the Written Law, or we reject Jewish law in its entirety."[116] This concept is to be applied even if the Rabbinical authorities are wrong! "A rare occasion may arise when the wise men will contend that the right side is the left one; even then, there is not

---

[113] Deuteronomy 17:11

[114] This word "*Halakah*" refers to Jewish legal rules. The word comes from the Hebrew verb "halak" which means "go" referring to the direction for people to go in their lives.

[115] Chill, The Mitzvot: The Commandments and their Rationale (Jerusalem: Keter Pub., 1974), pg.425

[116] ibid.

sufficient ground for defying their authority. They are overwhelmingly on the side of truth and their authority must not be compromised because of a rare error."[117]

This concept has always existed in Judaism and we even find Jesus referring to it in the New Testament. While Jesus did not always agree with the things that the religious scholars in his time said and did, he still urged the people (including his own disciples) in that time to follow the teachings of these recognized authorities. He said: "Then spoke Jesus to the crowds and to his disciples, saying, 'The scribes and the Pharisees sit on the seat of Moses: all things therefore whatever they tell you, do and keep:"[118] We find Jesus not only speaking about the authority the Rabbis had, he acted based upon their authority as well. We can see this in how Jesus dealt with a religious requirement that the authorities (the people who represented the official legally authorized Rabbinical authorities) demanded he perform. It is recorded in the Gospel of Matthew. "And when they came to Capernaum, they that received the half shekel came to Peter, and said, does not your teacher pay the half shekel? He said, Yes." Jesus then spoke to Peter and gave him a parable about being God's son, but he also instructed him to go fishing to obtain a fish which would have the "shekel" in its' mouth which he was then to give to the authorities. Jesus pointed out to Peter that since he was God's son, he didn't actually have to pay this half-shekel, but because the authorities, who God had put in place since the time of Moses, demanded it, he paid it because they had the divinely mandated Biblical authority at that time.[119]

In closing, it is clear that Jewish Rabbinical scholars have the authority to interpret and apply the religious teaching they have received from Moses' time and to modify and adjust those teachings as they see fit within their recognized systems of authority. They, of course, do not have the

---

[117] ibid., pg. 426
[118] Matthew 23:1-2
[119] Matthew 17:24-27

authority to change the Biblical texts, but they do have the authority to interpret those texts in light of the circumstances in which a matter is under discussion and their interpretations should be followed and accepted as binding rules. It is through this system that Judaism maintains a coherent religious system with recognized authorities that can legally interpret the rules that religious Jews are required to adhere to today. These also include those having to do with smacking and discipline.[120]

This methodology is clearly shown in the important book "To Kindle a Soul: Ancient Wisdom for Modern Parents and Teachers" by Rabbi Lawrence Kelemen. Rabbi Kelemen shows how this way of arriving at authoritative religious teachings relates to smacking children. He says: "Today, those most enthusiastic about corporal punishment often cite the Bible as their authority: 'He that spares the rod hates his child.'[121] They argue that this verse demands that we hit our children. However, traditional Jewish scholars never accept verses just at face value. Every verse must be understood in context, taking into account every other biblical passage and the entire corpus of Judaism's ancient oral tradition."[122]

In closing, it is helpful to consider the depth and breadth of the scholarship available from traditional Jewish sources. By doing this, we avail ourselves of a literal treasure trove of wisdom, knowledge and understanding.

---

[120] For more information about the rules and regulations governing the whole system of approaching corporal punishment from the Jewish perspective, I once again urge the reader to get the book mentioned in endnote number one for a full and comprehensive examination of this complex issue.

[121] Proverbs 13:24

[122] Kelemen, To Kindle a Soul: Ancient Wisdom for Modern Parents and Teachers," Targum Press: 2001, pg. 142.

3

The legal context of the book of Proverbs

Now, let us look at the legal context of the book of Proverbs. Unfortunately, this subject is rarely entertained in most circles of Christian scholarship that are advocating smacking. The advocates of smacking create the context and understanding for their readers or religious students seemingly without considering the orientation or world-view of the writer of the original books themselves. A teaching has developed around the book of Proverbs that portrays this volume as presenting God's timeless wisdom to mankind which is always to be applied without any real context. Any person can open up the Bible to the book of Proverbs and simply read therein and apply all of these statements exactly and without any real application of rules for interpretation. With this type of a teaching in existence developing a dialogue with individuals espousing this position is very difficult because they are simply adhering to what is written in the Bible.

Scholars have recognized the danger of not placing this book in its proper context prior to interpretation. The English scholar, Dr. E.W. Bullinger, in his Companion Bible pointed this out in regard to the book of Proverbs. He said: "This book makes no claim to unity of authorship; it is avowedly a collection, and includes the work of others beside Solomon the King. Hence, though in some sections there may be wisdom of a general order, in others one may find cautions and counsels which were intended for a particular individual, and not for 'all sorts and conditions of men'; and which, therefore, are not abstract Wisdom in the sense implied by most

50

expositors of the book."[123] This appendix shows the common error that many religious expositors of this volume have fallen into. They have interpreted this volume literalistically and with no applicable context and herein lay one of the biggest problems in the smacking debate.

Commenting on this idea, Dr. Randall Heskett, in his article on Proverbs 23:13,14 comments on this same issue. "it is sad that many people assert their right to spank their children because 'the Bible' offers a warrant to do so. Yet they do not understand how to read the proverbs wisely. They interpret the Bible literalistically without hearing its literal sense, whereby the text is held together by its subject matter, namely the gospel of Jesus Christ."[124] Dr. Heskett shows it is essential to interpret the Proverbs in light of the revelation of the gospel of Jesus Christ and the message of God's grace to mankind. Most Christians would agree with this assertion, but the erroneous concept that this book of Proverbs contains timeless wisdom to be applied universally to all without any interpretation of the data based upon the cultural context or in light of the teachings of Jesus Christ revealed in the New Testament, affects how Christians apply and interpret this book.

To understand the book of Proverbs it is essential to orient the text to the reader. At this point, let us look at the legal context in which we find the book of Proverbs coming into existence. By understanding this fact, a person is well positioned to undertake a discussion of this fascinating and ancient volume.

The Legal orientation of King Solomon and King Hezekiah

King Solomon and King Hezekiah are two people who are specifically mentioned as authoring or editing sections of the book of Proverbs in which we find many of the texts specifically related to smacking.

---

[123] Bullinger, Companion Bible, Appendix 74, pg. 109.
[124] Dr. Randall Heskett, Proverbs 23:13,14, *Interpretation Journal*, April 2001, pg. 181.

King Solomon is identified as the primary author of this volume.[125] It is clear from the Bible that Solomon himself knew many proverbs. According to the Bible, Solomon "spake three thousand proverbs."[126] The book of Proverbs itself only contains 915 verses and many of the proverbs found therein occupy more than one verse.

Solomon is identified as the principal author. He is specifically designated as the author of the section of the book of Proverbs from Chapters 10:1 to 22:16.[127] Solomon's proverbs are also specifically found in another section of the book. It is from Proverbs 25:1 to 29:27. We know this because we find the following statement referring to this fact. It reads: "These are the proverbs of Solomon, which the men of Hezekiah king of Judah copied out.[128] So, we know that this book came together under Solomon, but it also was added to in the time of Hezekiah, who lived about 200 years later than Solomon.

We know also for a fact that some sections of the book are even older and were collated and collected by the ancient Hebrews and placed in the book. Some of these writings have been found in the ancient collections of writings coming from ancient Egypt.[129] [Some people contend that because of this it makes sense to take these Scriptures with a grain of salt. I don't agree with this thesis. The 915 verses that make up the book of Proverbs may not have been divine Scripture prior to the time they were put together, but after they were put together and placed in the Bible, they are now as much Holy Scripture as the Gospels themselves.]

It has been pointed out also that Proverbs 1:7 through Chapter 9 may have been authored by the ancient patriarch Joseph.[130] This idea has

---

[125] Proverbs 1:1
[126] I King 4:32
[127] See Proverbs 10:1 which starts with the following statement; "The proverbs of Solomon."
[128] Proverbs 25:1
[129] See Ancient Near Eastern Texts, p.428b
[130] See Ernest L. Martin, *The Writings of Joseph in Egypt* (Pasadena: Foundation for Biblical Research: 1977).

52

merit particularly with the textual focus in this section about avoiding adultery, something Joseph was recognized for in Biblical history. Now, that we have the time frame and know that this book came from the times of Solomon and Hezekiah, what was the legal orientation of these two men during the times in which they lived? By answering this question, we can better understand the legal context of Proverbs.

Now, let us look at the legal orientation of King Solomon. Just before his father, King David, passed away, David met with his son, who would become the next king and gave him the following advice. The Bible says: "Now the days of David drew near that he should die; and he charged Solomon his son, saying, I go the way of all the earth: be thou strong therefore, and show thyself a man; and keep the charge of the LORD your God, to walk in his ways, to keep his statutes, and his commandments, and his judgments, and his testimonies, as it is written in the Law of Moses, that you may prosper in all that you do, and where ever you turn yourself."[131]

What we see clearly from this verse is that the legal orientation that David commanded his son to follow was that found in the "Law of Moses."[132] We find later that Solomon was condemned because he did not follow this Law of Moses. Note this: "And the LORD was angry with Solomon, because his heart was turned from the Lord GOD of Israel, who had twice appeared to him and had commanded him concerning this thing, that he should not go after other gods: but he (Solomon) kept not that which the LORD commanded. So that the LORD said to Solomon, 'Since this is your mind, and thou has not kept my covenant and my statutes, which I have commanded you, I will surely rend the kingdom from you and give it to your servant.'"[133] The context shows that Solomon violated the first of the Ten

---

[131] I King 1 2:1-3
[132] ibid.
[133] I Kings 11:9-11

Commandments[134] by worshipping other gods.[135] These commands were first revealed to Moses, so Solomon violated the very Law of Moses that his father, King David, demanded that he keep.

It is clear from this text that the legal orientation of King Solomon and his father, King David, were the same. Both of them were adherents to the legal requirements of the Law of Moses. That is exactly what the texts teach and there are several other such texts in other sections of the Bible concerning these two men and their adherence to the legal system founded by God through Moses. The point is, the legal orientation of these two men affected everything they did and everything they wrote. Without understanding the orientation of the writer, we are in the dark about how we as readers today are to orient ourselves toward the text.

As I mentioned King Hezekiah previously, what was his legal orientation during the time he lived because it was his men who, under his instructions, copied out some of the other proverbs of Solomon (and today we find these writings in the book of Proverbs)? King Hezekiah was 25 years old when he began to reign as king.[136] He did that which was correct in God's eyes.[137] His first actions involved removing illegal religious places of worship as defined in the Law of Moses.[138] He trusted in God and his actions were characterized as being unlike any ruler in Judaea before his time.[139] "For he held fast to the LORD, and departed not from following Him, but kept His commandments, which the LORD commanded Moses."[140]

So, we can see a common thread of belief and legal orientation among these men who were involved in the writing and construction of the book of Proverbs. What these texts show is that the principal revealed

---

[134] Exodus 20: 1-7
[135] I Kings 11:4-8
[136] I Kings 18:1
[137] I Kings 18:3
[138] I Kings 18:4
[139] I Kings 18:5
[140] I Kings 18:7

authors of Proverbs had an orientation toward the Law of Moses. This Law of Moses is found in the first five books of the Bible and concerns the laws revealed to Moses by God which were the religious and civil law that has existed since the time of Moses and has been legally binding for Israelites and adherents to Judaism since that time. This system was also the legal system that was in force during the time when Jesus Christ lived.[141]

How does this relate to people today understanding the book of Proverbs? The point is, the book of Proverbs can only be appreciated and correctly understood in an environment where the Law of Moses is the legal orientation. Without this understanding, the book has no real context. Remove it from this context and you have chaos. This also makes sense even from the very beginning of the book of Proverbs. The first verse of the book says: " The proverbs of Solomon, the son of David, King of Israel…"[142] Solomon, in the first proverb also urges his readers to "My son, hear the instruction of thy father, and do not forsake the law of your mother."[143] The word for "law" is the Hebrew word "*torah*" which is used numerous times to describe the "law of Moses."[144] The point is, all of the information that you find in the book of Proverbs was produced within a legal and religious environment where the Law of Moses was the governing religious system.

Biblical scholars have long pointed this fact out. "The wisdom, therefore, and instruction, of which so much is said in the book of Proverbs, is to be understood chiefly of moral and religious discipline, imparted, according to the direction of the Law [of Moses], by the teaching and under the example of parents."[145]

---

[141] See Mark 1:44 and several dozen other similar passages.
[142] Proverbs 1:1
[143] Proverbs 1:8
[144] See Joshua 8:31, 8:32, II Kings 14:6
[145] See Proverbs 1:2; 1:8; 2:2; 2:10; 4:1; 4:4; 4:20; 8:1; 9:1; 9:10; 12;1; 16:22; 27:24; 31 and Mc'Lintock and Strong's *"Cyclopedia of Biblical, Ecclesiastical & Theological Literature,"* article,'Education, Hebrew,' vol. III, 61.

So how do we understand the Book of Proverbs today?

How does this affect the way in which we understand the teachings in the book of Proverbs? It affects them greatly because the teachings that we find in the book of Proverbs are not specifically Christian in orientation; they are oriented toward the Law of Moses. And why not? This is the exact orientation that the author of the book intended in the first place.

Note the following: "The aim of the proverbs included here is to make men know wisdom: when that is accomplished, it is hoped that men will do that which is right. As Crawford H. Toy[146] points out, the emphasis throughout this book [of Proverbs] is "on the intellectual recognition of the right as the basis of the good life is allied to the Socratic conception of morality, which is simply that if one knows what is right, he will do what is right. Conversion, or the change of heart, is not found in Proverbs."[147]

That is right! Conversion, or repentance, which means a change of heart, is something that Christians find being taught at the beginning of the Gospel message of Jesus Christ revealed first in the teachings of John the Baptist and subsequently by Christ himself.[148] Proverbs, as a doctrinal statement of belief has nothing to do with repentance, a changed heart or conversion. It has to do with the acquisition of knowledge as the key to right behaviour.[149] Knowledge is also a key aspect of law. You must know the law to keep the law.

Now, are we here saying that Proverbs is not Holy Scripture? No! In no way! Proverbs is a holy book to be sure as are all of the books of the Hebrew Bible (the Old Testament), but as I just mentioned, the idea of "conversion" is not found in this book. Conversion of the heart is the central doctrine of Christianity. This is why Christ came to earth in the first place to save people. People know what is right, but they cannot do what is right

---

[146] Crawford Toy is a Christian scholar who wrote one of the most respected commentaries on the book of Proverbs.
[147] The Interpreters Bible (New York: Abingdon Press), vol. IV, pg. 780.
[148] See Matthew 2 &3, Luke 3 and Mark 1.
[149] Proverbs 1

perfectly. If they could, there would be no need for a saviour. This is the exact teaching given by the Apostle Paul in the book of Romans. Paul lamented the fact that while he indeed knew the law backwards and forwards, but he found in himself an inability to keep that law perfectly.[150] He now had something much better. The idea that man repents and turns from sin and accepts Jesus Christ is the key to the Gospel message. Without repentance, or "changing your heart," you can be the wisest person in the world and you can know what is right, but knowing what is right will not save one from sin. Knowing wisdom is one thing, but knowing Jesus Christ is another.

It is most important to realize that if we do not recognize this fact, we will continue to perpetuate the error that many are engaging in today stating that the texts in the book of Proverbs concerning smacking children are binding and in force today upon Christians. It is agreed that they are binding and in force today as much as they ever were since Solomon wrote the book and since God delivered the Law to Moses on Mount Sinai. The only point that needs to be made is that, as a Christian, one is no longer under the rules laid down in the Law of Moses because as Christians we now have a different law: the Law of Christ. This law is found in Galatians 5:23.

In closing, let us be very careful to apply the sections of the Bible that are directed *to* us and *for* us. The whole of the Bible is for our admonition, but the whole of the Bible is not directed to us. Just as God told Jonah to go and preach to the people of Nineveh, does that mean that every person named Jonah today needs to pack up his belongings and go to Nineveh today? The book of Jonah was directed to a particular "Jonah" and at a particular time. The same thing applies to the book of Proverbs. It is there for our admonition, but the entirety of the book must be interpreted in light of the Gospel message of salvation by grace.[151]

---

[150] Romans 7:14-25
[151] "Proverbs 23:13-14" by Dr. Randall Heskett in *Interpretation Journal*, Apr. 2001, pgs.181-4.

Let us all seek to follow the example given by Paul who said a Christian should be "a worker that needs not to be ashamed, rightly dividing the word of truth."[152] The truth can be divided. All truth is truth, to whom it is directed at the time it is given. Let us find our truth for today and apply it to our lives especially where vitally important questions regarding the upbringing, guidance and future of our children and our world are concerned.

---

[152] II Timothy 2:15

4

The gender focus of the book of Proverbs

One of the most interesting aspects of the religious system outlined in the Old Testament is the different statuses assigned to men and women. Whether you agree with it or not, whether it applies today or not, this doesn't matter. What is important to understand is that these differences were real in ancient times and they definitely affected the way that people in that time looked at the world.

How does this subject relate to the Biblical argument concerning smacking of children? The fact is, it relates very much because it is in Proverbs that we find the primary texts used by most people to justify smacking as an appropriate tool for child rearing. The majority of the argument in favour of smacking children (from the religious point of view) is primarily based on using the textual evidence in Proverbs. A person only need examine the books or other resources created by smacking proponents to demonstrate this fact without any doubt. If we did not find the texts in the book of Proverbs relating to smacking, there would be no need for this research. Without the statements from the book of Proverbs, anyone who is advocating smacking will lose virtually all of their primary evidence in favour of this argument.

The book of Proverbs: A background

The book of Proverbs is one of the most interesting books in the Bible. In it we find some of the oldest sections in the whole Bible. People have been quoting it for centuries. We even find that some sections of this book have been found in sources outside of the Bible. A whole section of this book has been found in an ancient book from Egypt known as "The Instruction of Amen-em-opet." The section of the book of Proverbs found in this book is from chapter 22:22 to 24:22. These thirty verses that are found in our modern Bibles date to very early periods.[153] There are other texts from outside of the Bible that also feature sections of the book of Proverbs in them.[154] This is an extremely old book. There is no doubt that this book contains information in it from numerous international sources that were collected and collated into one key volume representing the best proverbial sayings from the ancient world.

The first question we have to ask about this book is its context relative to the other Biblical books.[155] Do we find this book positioned in the Bible in a place that will help to understand its' contents? In essence, does the context we find the book in make a difference in the way we interpret it? The answer to this question is "yes." The main reason is that information found in the Bible is not just haphazardly put here and there. It is placed where it is for a reason and in a context. Let us look at two examples that show this clearly. Let us look at an example demonstrating this.

---

[153] Ancient Near Eastern Texts, pg.421-4

[154] ibid., pg. 428b – There is a text known as "The Words of Ahiqar" which is written in a language very similar to Hebrew (Aramaic) and the text dates to a period about 500 years before Christ. This section actually concerns one of the key texts related to smacking children: Proverbs 23:13-14.

[155] I have already dealt with the legal context of the book of Proverbs in another section of this volume.

Context is important

First, there is a context to the information placed in the Bible. It is placed where it is for a reason. This must be the case because we actually find the same information, word for word, quoted in one section of the Bible and mentioned in another section. Now if we were only concerned with the raw information itself, this would not be needed. However, we find that the information that was placed in the Bible was placed there for a reason and there is even a reason why repeated information is placed in certain sections.

This phenomenon is particularly evident in the book of Psalms. Look at Psalm 14 and Psalm 53. They are practically the same. Also Psalm 70 is parallel with Psalm 40:13-17. Note also that Psalm 60:9-12 is the same as Psalm 108:10-13. While no one knows the exact reason for this arrangement, it must be that there is a key behind this design. There is something more to this matter than simply rehearsing information.

One of the key teachings we have to understand from these texts that there is a design involved here. Not only do we see design in the phenomenon of repeating information, we also see other designs in the positioning of books. Sixtus Senensis, the medieval Jewish scholar commented on this: "As with the Hebrew [language] there are twenty-two letters, in which all that can be said and written is comprehended, so there are twenty-two books in which are contained all that can be known and uttered of divine things."[156] This idea is also further emphasized in the fact that we find the feature of the Bible acrostic being used to show order regarding information. A good example of this is Psalm 119, which has 176 verses, divided into groupings of eight verses each. Each verses begins with a different Hebrew letter so the 22 letters in the Hebrew language each have eight verses bearing a letter in the first verse in this Psalm. We also even find

---

[156] *A General Introduction to the Old Testament*, vol. 1, pg. 87 by William H. Green

this phenomenon taking place in the last 22 verses of Proverbs 31 that describes a virtuous woman.

What this information shows is that there is a design feature in place that has to be taken into account in interpreting these books. Not only do we find these design features which are mentioned here in evidence, there are others. One in particular concerns a specific design feature related to gender. This design feature actually affects how we interpret the book of Proverbs. Let us look at it here.

Wisdom literature

The book of Proverbs is a part of a group of books in the Bible generally referred to as "Wisdom literature." There are two other books that specifically fall into this category and they are the book of Psalms and the book of Job. Now it is very interesting that in the original Hebrew order of the books of the Bible, we find these three books in order forming an actual collection of their own. This ancient order preserved in Hebrew bible versions is only different as far as the order of the books that we find in Protestant Bible versions. The books are the same, only the order and numbering is different.[157] These three books, Psalms, Proverbs and Job, actually begin a section in the Bible known as the Holy Writings.[158] Jesus referred to this idea when he mentioned the three divisions of the Hebrew Bible known in ancient times as the "Law, the Prophets and the Psalms."[159]

Now, these three books have a number of similar characteristics, but in this discussion, I wish to focus solely on one. It is the fact that these books exhibit a common orientation to issues that are of interest to and almost

---

[157] A good example of this is the Hebrew Bible's reference to the book of Chronicles. This single book in the Hebrew Bible is made up of two books in our English Bible. They are First and Second Chronicles. These two books in our modern versions originally were numbered only as one book in the Hebrew Bible and this continues to this present day. See the appendix in this book "The order of the Hebrew Bible books versus the order found in Protestant Bible versions."

[158] Greek: *Hagiographia*

[159] Luke 24:44-45

solely concern men! This may seem like an odd statement at first, but if a person is willing to look closely at the data that are found in these books, one cannot help but to come away with such a feeling that they are decidedly masculine in theme and character. Not only are all the authors of these books men, but the themes that the books feature are also definitely more masculine in nature. Let us consider some of the evidence that makes this clear.

Looking at the first book in the Hebrew order of this small three-book collection of wisdom literature we find the book of Psalms. First, look at the people involved in writing the Psalms. They are David, Solomon, Moses, Asaph, Korah, Ethan, Jeremiah, etc.[160] Note that in the Bible we have Psalm type sections written or sung by women, but they are not included in the book of Psalms because of its masculine orientation.[161] These Psalms (or songs) were spiritual songs sung in the Holy Temple in Jerusalem by priests, who were men and contributed to the spiritual system of the Israelite religion.[162] Additionally, in the Bible the singing of spiritual music is something that is decidedly masculine in nature. Note that singers and prophets who also engaged in singing were men. Many of these singers were also priests of the family of Aaron or Levites and had a focus of their ministry towards the Holy Temple.[163]

Now, the book of Psalms begins with the statement: "Happy is the **man** who walks not in the counsel of the ungodly."[164] If one will survey this

---

[160] King David wrote the first 72 Psalms. (See Psalm 72:20) Psalm 72 was written either by or for King Solomon. Moses wrote Psalm 90. Asaph wrote numerous Psalms such as those from 73-83. Korah wrote many Psalms such as those found in 84-88. Ethan wrote the major part of Psalm 89. A careful examination of Psalm 119 with a comparison with the book of Lamentations almost certainly points to Jeremiah as the author.

[161] See Exodus 15:21 which is sung by Miriam and resembles a very short Psalm. Note also Judges 5 which is a type Psalm sung by Deborah and Barak. Finally, note the Psalm sung by Hannah in I Samuel 2:1-10.

[162] I Chronicles 25:2-5

[163] See I Samuel 16:16 and also see I Samuel 10:5-7

[164] Psalm 1:1

book, it will be found that the subject matter is decidedly masculine in nature and tone.

Next in the order of the Hebrew Bible, we find the Book of Proverbs. Before we look at Proverbs, however, let us first consider the next book in the Hebrew Bible order. This is the book of Job. Job was a wise man dwelling in the land of Uz. (or a Wizard of Oz – that is another story)[165] The book of Job features speeches by five men and then a final speech by the LORD, who is always spoken of as a masculine being.[166] The subject matter concerns a great wealthy and wise man that had to deal with tragedy in his life and how he came to accept it and understand God and his teachings in a clearer way. The whole orientation of this book is masculine. Now, before I begin the discussion on the book of Proverbs, I would like to point something out. God did not forget women. This is very important to understand as women played a key role in the religion of the ancient Hebrews. We will see the theme of femininity playing a key role in the orientation of the next five books in the Hebrew order of the Biblical books. Let us look at these now.

The Biblical collection devoted to feminine themes

As I mentioned, the Hebrew order of the books, which is different from our Protestant Bible versions only in the order of the books (not the content) features a number of books that are in order and feature decidedly feminine themes. We have looked at the masculine focus of Psalms, Proverbs and Job. Now, the books that feature this feminine focus are the next five books that we find after Job. They are known in by the Hebrew term *Megillot*[167] which is

---

[165] Job 1:1

[166] For clear evidence of this, see Proverbs 8 where the LORD is pictured as a masculine being complemented by the feminine Wisdom, a very mysterious and thought provoking association.

[167] The Hebrew word *Megillot* in English means "Scrolls." In this case, it refers to these five scrolls that we read at the festival times of ancient Israel. These festival periods were Passover when the Song of Songs was read, Ruth which was read at Pentecost, Lamentations which was read on the destruction date of the

itself expressed in the feminine gender. They are Songs of Songs, Ruth, Lamentations, Ecclesiastes and Esther. Let us look at the evidence for this feminine focus.

First, note the opening to the Song of Songs. The first voice in the book (after the introduction) speaking is a woman. She says: "Let him kiss me with the kisses of his mouth."[168] This book is a romantic poem between a woman and a man. This is a very romantic volume that was read as a dramatic opera. This volume constantly refers to feminine themes.

Next, comes the book of Ruth. Ruth was the great grandmother of King David.[169] The feminine orientation of Ruth is obvious. It is the story of a woman, a foreigner who embraced the Jewish faith, who became one of the most important women in the history of ancient Israel. Her story was so important that a book was written about it and placed in the Bible. In this book, we find numerous customs and rituals associated with male/female relationships, but it is written in a decidedly feminine orientation.

Following Ruth, we find the book of Lamentations. It is not often recognized as a book oriented towards the feminine, but look at the first few verses of the book itself. "How does the city sit solitary, that was full of people! How is **she** become as a **widow, she** who was great among the nations, was a **princess** among the provinces, how is **she** become a vassal. **She** weeps sore in the night, and **her** tears are upon **her** cheek. Among all **her** lovers **she** has none to comfort **her**. All **her** friends have betrayed **her**, they have become **her** foes."[170]

Can a text be any clearer to illustrate this feminine orientation? What we also have to understand about the book of Lamentations is that it

---

Temple, the ninth of the Hebrew month of Ab, Ecclesiastes was read at the feast of Tabernacles and finally, Esther was read at Purim.

[168] Song of Songs 1:2

[169] Ruth 3:17-18

[170] Lamentations 1:1-2

represents the death of the nation of Israel and in Hebrew culture, and it was women who most often did the lamenting over the dead.[171]

The next book in the Hebrew order is Ecclesiastes. It may stick out as an unfeminine book, but we must look under the surface here to see the femininity of this book. When one truly analyses this work, this is a treatise dealing with the deep mysteries and life from the highest of philosophical aspects. The author was without question supremely equated with the virtue of wisdom. Wisdom, as demonstrated numerous times in Proverbs, is a feminine virtue.[172] Some scholars point out that this term "*kohelet*" is in the feminine gender in Hebrew and literally translated it means "Congregation of Women."[173] Could this essay, while being given by a man, have been inspired from the highest of feminine virtues, Wisdom? It could be. We do find this work among other books exhibiting feminine characteristics.

The last book of this feminine section is the book of Esther. This book is the story of a young Jewish woman whose wisdom and femininity saved the whole of Jewish civilization during the time of the Persian Empire. This story must be considered an inspiration to all women no matter where they are or what social position in which they find themselves.

Now that we have seen the masculinity exhibited in the books of Psalms, Proverbs and Job and the femininity of Song of Songs, Ruth, Lamentations, Ecclesiastes and Esther, we can now see the importance and consideration of these gender issues that must be taken into account when interpreting these books. This is especially the case for the book of Proverbs. This is because the book of Proverbs is an extremely masculine book. If we do not take this fact into account, our whole conception of the book as a whole could be misguided. By taking into consideration where among the collection of books that we find this book, this will assist us greatly in

---

[171] Note Mark 16:10 which is one example of many that could be given concerning women and lamenting.

[172] See Proverbs 1:20,24; 8:1;32-36; 9:1-11)

[173] See *Restoring the Original Bible*, Ernest L. Martin (ASK Publications: Portland: 1994), pg. 131.

interpreting the data found in that book. Seeing the larger context of the book, let us now listen to the tone of Proverbs itself. This will have a decided impact on how we further consider the statements given in this most difficult book.

The Masculine context and tone of the book of Proverbs

As I have shown in the previous paragraph, the book of Proverbs appears in a context surrounded by other books exhibiting masculine themes. The book itself, however, without ambiguity exudes masculinity. The points I wish to make are these: the information found in the book of Proverbs is directed to men. It shows men how to conduct their lives. It shows men how to deal with family and society and it also shows kings (who in Israelite culture were always men) how to deal with their subjects.

The masculine tone of the book of Proverbs commences at the very beginning. Before any proverbial teachings start, the author points out to whom the book is directed. The book begins with the following opening statement which orients the reader for the rest of the discussion: "The proverbs of Solomon, son of David, king of Israel: For the knowledge of wisdom and correction, for discerning the sayings of intelligence: for receiving of correction of prudence, righteousness and justice and equity; for giving to the simple shrewdness, to the **young man** knowledge and discretion. A wise **man** will hear and will increase learning, and a discreet **man** wise counsels will acquire."[174]

From the book's beginning the author makes a precise distinction whom the information is directed. This book is designed for the young man to give that young man discretion and the information is also for the man who is already wise and wishes to become wiser still. That young man may also be a ruler to whom large segments of the book are directed. The author cannot seemingly make the direction any clearer.

---

[174] Proverbs 1:1-5

This is a particularly important point to understand. Note also that when the author uses the phrase "young man," this in Hebrew is the word "*na'ar*." This phrase refers to the stage in life known as the teenage or young adult years. The writer could have used any word describing men to introduce this book, but this particular word was chosen.

This choice also makes perfect sense when one considers the subject matter of the book as a whole. (This will be discussed shortly.) Frankly stated, discussions put forth in this book require a certain level of age to be present to appreciate them. It is simply impossible for a 7 or 8 year old to appreciate the importance of avoiding adultery or recognizing the importance of marrying the right woman, being honest in business, saving money for the future and understanding complex comparisons such as being wise like animals. Young boys are more interested in fun and games rather than seriously thinking through elements of wisdom.

The point is, this book is not designed for young men below the teenage years and that is what the opening statement is indicating. It is in these periods when the adult awareness's begin to develop and when one begins to think about marriage and family. It is during this period when such advice makes the best sense and that is what we have given to us in the book of Proverbs. Attempting to communicate such ideas to young children will find an unready audience. In actual fact, some of the subject matter in the book of Proverbs is simply not appropriate for young children. For example, the subject of adultery is not an acceptable subject to discuss with a six year old. I think this is obvious to all so further discussion on this point is not necessary.

It must be admitted at this point that the Hebrew language only has two genders: masculine and feminine. So can we not say when it says "young man" that it really means young person (of either sex)? Some may make this assertion, but we will see that the written evidence for such a suggestion is simply not available when one considers the subject matter of this book as whole. Let us see how this is the case.

The next point to show that this book as a whole is directed only to men, and young men in particular, is found in the first division of the book. The reader encounters the phrase "My son" as a transitional phrase eleven times in the first nine chapters of this book.[175] Once again, it might be pointed out that this phrase could simply be translated as "my child" regardless of the sex, but once again this point cannot be justified from the texts. The reason for this is that the individual speaking is a father and the subject matter of the discussion is clearly oriented to that father's male child.[176]

Let us notice this fact clearly demonstrated. Notice the following text: "To rescue you from the **woman** that is a stranger, from the **female** unknown, who with **her** speech seduces."[177] This father is telling his son to avoid strange inappropriate women. This must be considered fine advice in any age and for any sex as any caring father would also advise his daughter to avoid unacceptable male partners.

Note also the following: "For with sweet droppings drip the lips of **her** that is a stranger, and smoother than oil is **her** mouth."[178] The fatherly advice continues: "Keep far from **her** your way, and do not go near the opening of **her** house."[179] Additionally, look at this: "Wherefore should you stray, my son, with a strange **woman**? or embrace the bosom of a **woman** unknown?"[180]

We can continue to read of this young man and how he is continually advised to avoid inappropriate women. Now is it to be construed that the author dislikes or is demeaning women here? It really does not seem so. However, he is advising his son to avoid the snare of adultery. Look at the

---

[175] These texts are found in 1:8; 1:10; 2:1; 3:1; 3:11; 3:21; 4:20; 6:1; 6:3; 6:20 and 7:1.
[176] Proverbs 1:8
[177] ibid., 2:16
[178] ibid., 5:3
[179] ibid., 5:8
[180] ibid., 5:20

following that shows this: "Can a **man** snatch up fire in **his** bosom, and **his** clothes not be burned? So **he** that goes in unto **his** neighbour's wife, no **man** shall be guiltless who touches her ... **He** that commits adultery with a woman lacks sense, a destroyer of **his** own life is **he** that does it."[181]

I think most would say this is fine advice for all. What else does the father suggest? "Drink you water out of your own cistern, and flowing streams out of the middle of your own well. Let not your fountains flow over abroad in the streets, dividings of waters. Let them be for yourself alone, and for strangers with you. Let your wellspring be blessed and get your joy from the wife of your youth: A loving hind! A graceful doe! Let her bosom content you at all time. And in her love may you stay evermore."[182]

The point here is clear. "Son, get married at a good young age, rejoice with your wife and don't commit adultery." I must say again that there is a bias toward men in this book. This is particularly so in this first division. Let us now consider further data in the rest of the book to see this point fully illustrated.

There is a more masculine emphasis in the book of Proverbs when it comes to the discussion of wives and women. I only point out these texts as evidence in regard to my thesis here. Wives are considered a blessing for husbands: "Who has found a wife has found a blessing, and has obtained favour from the LORD."[183] We see a similar theme echoed in the following statement: "House and substance are an inheritance from one's father, but from the LORD comes a wife who is prudent."[184] Foolish children and contentious wives are lamented: "Engulfing ruin to his father is a son who is a dullard, and a continuous dripping are the contentions of a wife."[185]

Some may find these statements about women inappropriate for our modern world. In one way I agree, but I am quick to point out, with a sense

---

[181] ibid., 6:27-32
[182] ibid., 5:15-19
[183] ibid., 18:22
[184] ibid., 19:14
[185] ibid., 19:13

of humour, that if one accepts my thesis of the masculine orientation of Proverbs, it must then be admitted that when the book speaks of "fools" and "dullards" and those "lacking understanding" it is men who are being spoken of! So, in a sense, we see here, a fair treatment of both sexes.

For example, we see that an unchaste woman is spoken of as a "deep chasm."[186] But, what is the man, who finds himself in the embrace of a prostitute called? He is called a "simple one."[187] He is also called an "ox,"[188] and finally a "fool."[189] There is little favouritism directed at one sex or the other in this book. What are in evidence are strict social divisions of the sexes that were present in those times. Some may find these divisions repressive by modern standards, but it represents an error to judge the ancient Israelitish culture on the basis of our culture today. This is cultural relativism and such judgments are not helpful to anyone.

Finally, we can see a wonderful description of the virtuous woman.[190] In Chapter 31, here the virtuous woman is described as a wife, mother, businesswoman, physically fit and a merciful community activist. We see the righteous man exemplified in his seeking for wisdom, understanding and knowledge, practicing justice, knowing prudence, avoiding evil associations, saving for the future, speaking softly and a man who cares for his family and is totally faithful to his wife. These are just a few of the virtues that characterize the virtuous man as found in the book of Proverbs.

Application to the concept of smacking

After showing that the subject matter of this book is directed to men, what does this mean as far as the subject of smacking? The suggestion made here is that the Bible is teaching something that has been overlooked by many

---

[186] ibid., 23:27
[187] ibid., 7:7
[188] ibid., 7:22
[189] ibid., 7:23
[190] See all of Proverbs 31

Bible scholars and commentators. This is the fact that the texts in the book of Proverbs that speak of smacking with the rod apply only to the male, never to the female!

This may seem fantastic and absurd to some scholars and Bible teachers, but the evidence in this regard is quite compelling. The fact is, legally speaking men and women were treated differently among the Hebrew religion and culture and it is about time that those of us living in modern times recognized this fact and stop blindly applying texts that have no application to our modern existence outside of their original contexts and methodology of understanding. Let us consider this suggestion now.

Smacking only for the male sex?

The book of Proverbs speaks of the use of smacking in several places and in these texts; there is one thing in common. They all have a strong masculine bias. Because of the orientation of the book as a whole as well, could it be that the ancients only ever directed them to males? Based on my examination of the texts, this seems to be a plausible suggestion. This appears clearly to have been the intention of the writer of these texts. Let us consider some of this evidence.

Note the following: "In the lips of **him** that has understanding wisdom is found: but a rod is for the back of **him** that is void of understanding."[191] In this text in the original Hebrew, there is no ambiguity. If the author had intended both sexes to be spoken of, why did he not use the plural pronoun "them" instead of the singular masculine "him?" The use of the plural "them" would have included both sexes in the discussion.

Note also the following: "**He** that spares **his** rod, hates **his son**: but **he** that loves **him** carefully corrects **him**."[192]

Note the bolded words specifically pointed out here because they are very clear in the original Hebrew. The words are all in the third person

---

[191] Proverbs 10:13
[192] ibid., 13:24

singular masculine. If both sexes were intended by the author, he would have said: "He that spares his rod, hates his **children**: but he that loves **them** carefully corrects **them**." However, this is not the case. We find the author sticking with the third person singular masculine focus of the book throughout. This is because the overwhelming subject matter of this book is written about and for men. Dr. Randall Heskett also points out this idea of these texts being oriented solely for men.[193] Dr. Heskett is not alone in this opinion. Let us look at another scholarly opinion in this regard.

The book of Proverbs and its masculine orientation

The idea that the book of Proverbs is oriented towards men in particular is not only clearly revealed in the text of the book itself, but other scholars have also pointed this out. One important example of this can be found in the work of Dr. E. W. Bullinger.

Dr. Bullinger was a highly active conservative Bible scholar in England about 100 years ago. His chief accomplishment of many decades of Biblical research was the production of the *Companion Bible*. This Bible version is a monument to conservative Christian Bible scholarship. In this volume, Dr. Bullinger produced copious notes and added numerous appendices to help non-experts better understand the Holy Bible. It is in one of these appendices that we find a very important article about the book of Proverbs.

This appendix points out that the gender orientation of this book is decidedly masculine. "If the contents of sections one[194] and two[195] already described had been by Solomon, there would have been no need in this place for the introductory line 'The Proverbs of Solomon.' That mode of address

---

[193] See Heskett, *Interpretation Journal*, April 2001, Article "Proverbs *23:13-14*," pgs. 181-184.
[194] Proverbs 1:7-9:18
[195] Proverbs 10:1-22:16

is quite unlike that of section one,[196] with its second person of the pronoun; the proverbs are not spake to "my son," [as in Proverbs 1:7 to 9:18] but they mention "**he**" and "**him**," using generally the third person of the pronoun. [It is third person masculine also] Apparently, they continue to chapter 19:26, or thereabouts. **They were for men in general to learn**, and not for a prince or distinguished individual to learn. (as "my son.")[197]

Dr. Bullinger is not alone is his assertion that the book of Proverbs is squarely oriented towards the male gender. Dr. John J. Pilch, in an excellent article concerning the attitudes of ancient Israelites towards punishment, points out the following. "Most of the parenting advice in Sirach[198] and Proverbs concerns 'sons' or is addressed to males."[199] This is another proof to show that the book of Proverbs was written by men and was directed to men in general and younger men specifically.

Doesn't the Bible mean both sexes when it refers here to the male gender?

Some may say that both sexes are intended by the use of the singular pronoun and because Hebrew has no neuter gender, we are supposed to assume it means both. This may be, but why do we have to interpret the texts in this fashion? If it means "children" of both genders, why doesn't the text simply use the plural of "child," which is easy to construct in the Hebrew language and is done dozens of times in the Bible? Look at the following where the Bible makes use of the masculine and the feminine in the same texts and uses both the feminine and masculine pronouns: "and your sons and your

---

[196] Proverbs 1:7-9:18

[197] The Companion Bible, The Lamp Press: London, Appendix 74, pg. 109

[198] Sirach is a book that is a part of what is known as the Apocrypha. The subject of this book is that of wisdom and is similar to the book of Proverbs in subject matter. It is known by many names, but the most common one today is "*Ecclesiasticus.*" This volume is very old and is widely quoted in Jewish antiquity, but it is not a part of the Protestant canon of Holy Scripture.

[199] Dr. John J. Pilch, *"Beat his ribs while he is young" (Sirach 30:12): A window into the Mediterranean World*, Biblical Theology Bulletin, 1993. Georgetown University.

daughters shall prophesy; your old men shall dream dreams, your young men shall see visions."[200] This text is clear as it mentions both sons and daughters. Now, if sons and daughters are meant clearly in Proverbs, one seemingly has to read such an interpretation into the text without any Biblical textual authority.

To conclude this section, the gender orientation of the book of Proverbs is decidedly masculine. Any attempt to suggest or prove otherwise does serious violence to the data outlined in the whole of the book. It is therefore essential that we take this information into consideration when attempting to draw conclusions about the teachings given in this book. If we don't do this, we run the risk of missing out on what the true teachings of this book may be.

The point to this whole question comes down to this: Shouldn't we carefully consider the evidence and the data regarding such an important thing as raising our children and the proper way to train them and even to correct them? Don't we wish to communicate to them the concepts of love, unity, grace, peace, truth, non-violence and harmony? Should not our sole desire in raising our children be to come to know the fruits of the Holy Spirit of God that are universally recognized principles of goodness recognized by all faiths? These are: "Love, joy, peace, longsuffering, kindness, goodness, faithfulness, gentleness, self-control;"[201] One would think that virtually all parents would definitely answer these questions with a resounding "yes."

---

[200] Joel 3:1
[201] Galatians 5:22

5

The New Testament and the texts advocating smacking in the book of Proverbs

One of the most puzzling aspects of the whole argument concerning smacking is encountered when one looks at the data that are found in the New Testament. This collection of 27 books written by less than a dozen people features all of the teachings that make up the basis for the Christian faith.

When one looks at the New Testament, one finds numerous references to the Hebrew Bible (the Old Testament). The exact number of direct quotes and allusions from the Hebrew Bible to specific texts in the New Testament is over 200. Now among these quotes we find the book of Proverbs quoted directly 23 times in the New Testament. Because of the importance of the association between these books, let us look at each of these quotes and examine each context in which they refer to the book of Proverbs.

General Comments and Overview

To begin, there are a number of books (actually the majority of books) that do not quote the book of Proverbs directly even one time. These are Matthew, Mark, the book of Acts, I Corinthians, Galatians, Philippians, Colossians, I and II Thessalonians, I and II Timothy, Titus, Philemon, I, II and III John and Jude.

None of these books refer to any passage from the whole of the book of Proverbs. This is particularly important when you consider the contents of such books as the Pastoral Epistles of Saint Paul (First and Second Timothy, Titus and Philemon). These volumes were directed to pastors who had congregations and Paul never once related any teaching in any part of those books to any portion of the book of Proverbs. Now, I am not suggesting that Paul did not accept the whole of the book of Proverbs as inspired Scripture (because he quoted it in other sections of his works), however when you consider the subject matter of these four books, they contain numerous teachings on social issues and many of them relate to children,[202] but not only does Paul not quote any of the texts relating to smacking[203] he doesn't even refer to a single passage from the whole of the book of Proverbs. In First Timothy, Paul even refers to adults who were "chastened," but he doesn't use the same language when speaking about children.[204] Paul also doesn't refer to any text from Proverbs in II Thessalonians even though he discusses subjects relating to parents and children.[205]

Probably the most important example where Paul put parents on notice concerning their behaviour towards their children is found in his letter to the Colossians. He said: "Fathers, provoke not your children, that they be not discouraged."[206] [Could it be that Paul said this in response to the actions of some parents whose provocations against their children were leading them to discouragement?] This is the perfect point to raise the texts from Proverbs about smacking as a corollary to this thought, but this idea is nowhere to be found here or in the whole of the book of Colossians. In fact, the book of Colossians does not even quote the book of Proverbs directly one time.

---

[202] See I Timothy 3:4; 3:12 Titus 1:6.
[203] Proverbs 10:13; 13:24; 22:15; 23:13-14 and 29:15.
[204] I Timothy 1:20.
[205] II Thessalonians 2:7 and 2:11.
[206] Colossians 3:21

Finally, look at the example of the Gospels of Matthew and Mark. We find children to be a frequent topic of discussion,[207] but in both of these books, Proverbs is not directly quoted once.

Now, what about the books that do quote Proverbs? Let us look at the individual Scriptures and relate them to the book of Proverbs. First, let us look at the books of the New Testament, in order, which only quote Proverbs one time.

First, we have a reference in the book of Luke. This is as follows: "But when you are bidden, go and take the lowest place; that when he that hath bidden you comes, he shall say to you, Friend, go up higher: then shall you have glory in presence of all that sit at meat with you."[208] This text refers to a passage from Proverbs that mentions a similar thought.[209] This point is given in a parable of Jesus.

The book of James also only refers to the book of Proverbs one time in the five chapters. Speaking about adulteresses,[210] James said: "Wherefore it saith, God resists the proud, but gives grace to the humble."[211] This text refers to a specific proverb from Proverbs 3.[212] In both of these single examples, we find no reference to any of the Proverbs relating to smacking[213] nor do these texts even refer to children.

Next, we have the book of John that quotes Proverbs twice.[214] Neither of these quotes refers to any of the smacking texts or children either. The book of Romans quotes from Proverbs four times.[215] Again, none of these texts refer to smacking or children at all. The book of Second

---

[207] See Matthew 18:2,3,4,5; 19:13,14; Mark 9:36, 37; 10:13,14,15.
[208] Luke 14:10.
[209] Proverbs 25:6-7.
[210] See James 4:4.
[211] James 4:6.
[212] Proverbs 3:34.
[213] Proverbs 10:13; 13:24; 22:15; 23:13-14 and 29:15.
[214] John 1:1 quotes Proverbs 8:30 and John 3:13 quotes 30:4
[215] Romans 2:15, 11:14, 11:17 and 12:20 refer to Proverbs 1:16, 3:7, 3:4 and 25:21 respectively.

Corinthians refers to Proverbs three times.[216] Once again, none of these texts quote the Proverbs relating to smacking or children. These two epistles written by the Apostle Peter refer to Proverbs five times.[217] Repeating the same theme, none of these verses quotes the texts relating to smacking, nor do they refer to children. One does refer to the "children" of Abraham, but this is not referring to actual young people.[218] On the contrary, Peter urged his readers to "be fervent in your love among yourselves; for love covers a multitude of sins."[219] This would have been the perfect point to quote Proverbs 23:13-14 concerning the rod and sparing it, thus hating your son, but Peter was silent in this regard. The book of Revelation quotes Proverbs twice in the same chapter.[220] While one of the texts quoted in Proverbs does refer to children,[221] the text in the book of Revelation only quotes part of the text from Proverbs and does not include a reference inside the context or even remotely close to anything relating to children.[222] The text does not relate to children at all. Additionally, neither of the texts quotes the smacking texts from Proverbs concerning the rod. Finally, we have a text in Ephesians that mentions Proverbs as well,[223] but this text has nothing to do with children or the smacking texts either.

Finally, we have three texts remaining in the New Testament that do refer to children and discipline with direct reference to texts in the book of Proverbs. The first one is found in the book of Ephesians and it refers to two texts in the book of Proverbs in the same verse.[224] The book of Ephesians mentions the following: "And you, the fathers, provoke not your

---

[216] II Corinthians 3:3, 8:21 and 9:7 refer to Proverbs 3:3, 3:4 and 22:8 respectively.

[217] I Peter 2:17, 3:6, 4:8, 4:18 and II Peter 2:22 refer to Proverbs 24:21, 3:25, 10:12, 11:31 and 26:11 respectively.

[218] I Peter 3:6.

[219] I Peter 4:8.

[220] Revelation 3:14 and 3:19 refer to Proverbs 8:22 and 3:12.

[221] Proverbs 3:12.

[222] Revelations 3:17.

[223] Ephesians 5:18 refers to Proverbs 23:31.

[224] Ephesians 6:2 refers to Proverbs 2:2 and 3:11

children to anger: but be nourishing them up in the discipline and admonition of the Lord."[225] This quote refers directly to Proverbs 3:3 and 2:2. While it must be admitted that the verse in Proverbs 3:11 does have a similar word to describe "correction"[226] as we find in several of the smacking texts,[227] this word, correction, does not only mean correction received via the rod. This correction can be "heard,"[228] and "seen"[229] and "learned by incarceration."[230] In closing, had the Apostle Paul wished to refer his readers to the texts referring to smacking in this section (or any other of the contexts where he mentioned children or correction), he could have done so, but he did not.

The last two verses in the New Testament that quote the book of Proverbs are found in the twelfth chapter of the book of Hebrews.[231] One of these verses follows up on the first thought and does not specifically refer to disciplining children directly.[232] It is more of a comparison. The verse in question, which many Christian commentators point out does refer to physical punishment, is found in this section of the book of Hebrews. The texts says: "My son, despise not thou the chastening of the Lord, nor faint when thou art rebuked of him; For whom the Lord loveth he chasteneth, and scourgeth every son who he receiveth."[233]

The first thing to understand about this passage is that it refers to punishment, but does it refer specifically to punishment with a rod or specifically with any other instrument? No! Does this verse in the book of

---

[225] Ephesians 6:2

[226] Hebrew: *musar*

[227] See Proverbs 13:24, 22:15 & 23:13 that also use a Hebrew word "*musar*" for "correction."

[228] See Job 36:10, Proverbs 8:33, 13:1, 19:20 and Jeremiah 17:23.

[229] Proverbs 1:2. We read that the book of Proverbs was given to people to know instruction. To obtain the instruction the book speaks of, one has to read its contents.

[230] Proverbs 7:22 refers to receiving correction via the "stocks" and other translate this word as "chains." Incarceration was intended by the writer of Proverbs to teach correction.

[231] Hebrews 12:6 and 12:13 quote from Proverbs 3:11 and 4:26.

[232] Hebrews 12:13 referring to Proverbs 4:26.

[233] Hebrews 12:5-6

Hebrews refer back to any of the texts advocating smacking in the book of Proverbs?[234] No! Is the word rendered "scourging," which does refer to bodily punishment (and is used in that fashion in the New Testament[235]), ever used to describe actions taken against children? Not once.

When the New Testament mentions the word "scourging" and refers it back to the Old Testament book of Proverbs, does the word in Hebrew always mean bodily punishment or can it mean other things?[236] Yes, it can mean other things. In fact, when we look specifically at the context in Proverbs 3:11, we do not find the concept of "scourging," by means of a physical beating, in the text at all. What we do find is that the Hebrew word "*musar*" has a broad meaning and it does not only refer to physical punishment.

The important thing to understand concerning this passage is that we cannot put all of our theological eggs in one basket when considering this passage in the formulation of such an important Bible doctrine as something like smacking children. We need further confirmation of this idea in other Biblical passages in the New Testament, but, sadly, we don't have any such information concerning this subject. We have to understand that while all "scourging" is indeed punishment, not all punishment is "scourging." Punishment can be many things, but it isn't always understood as being with a rod or even taking place in regard to one's body. This is the exact teaching given in the contexts where we find the Hebrew word "*musar*"[237] used and without an application of these contexts as they appear in other sections of

---

[234] Proverbs 10:13; 13:24; 22:15; 23:13-14 and 29:15.
[235] John 19:1; Luke 18:33; Mark 10:34
[236] See Job 36:10, Proverbs 8:33, 13:1, 19:20 and Jeremiah 17:23; Proverbs 1:2. We read that the book of Proverbs was given to people to know instruction. To obtain the instruction the book speaks of, one has to read its contents. Proverbs 7:22 refers to receiving correction via the "stocks" and other translate this word as "chains." Incarceration was intended by the writer of Proverbs to teach correction.
[237] ibid.

the Bible (which helps us to define the Biblical meaning), we are not letting Scripture give us the meanings of the words that God is using.[238]

It is also quite problematic to base a teaching on one verse of Scripture.[239] The concept of seeking multiple witnesses is a Biblical concept and it should be utilized in the construction of Biblical doctrines especially where such important subjects such as the raising of youth are concerned.[240] This idea is also reinforced numerous times in the Hebrew Bible.[241] Here we are not debating how a Biblical name is pronounced or what day to attend church. Creating sound Bible doctrine in this regard is most important because the application of the doctrine will have profound effects on innocent children who cannot advocate for themselves.

So, in conclusion, what do the data show? In no instance does the New Testament quote from any of the texts that are used to demonstrate that smacking is valid for today. There is no instance in any of the New Testament's 27 books that specifically refers to a child receiving any bodily punishment. The evidence shows that the New Testament writers were quite familiar with the whole of the book of Proverbs and quoted from numerous sections of it, but wholly avoided any passage mentioning the rod. Because of these facts, anyone who seeks to advocate for the idea that smacking is a New Testament teaching is standing on shaky theological and Scriptural ground. This is the plain information we find in the Bible itself.

---

[238] See Isaiah 28:10-13

[239] ibid. & II Timothy 2:15 also speaks about "**rightly dividing** the word of truth" through study and examination. This verse strongly implies that the truth can also be "wrongly divided." Obviously, this is something we all wish to avoid. May God help us all in this regard.

[240] Matthew 18:16 & II Corinthians 13:1.

[241] Deuteronomy 17:6 & 19:15.

6

The New Testament references to physical punishment

As pointed out in the last chapter, specific references to smacking children are non-existent in the New Testament. We do, however, find references to physical beatings of a bodily nature. Let us look at these now.

While numerous passages mention "beating," "stripes" and similar such events, most of these passages refer to bodily chastisements that do not involve the rod. These beatings refer to people, especially to Jesus Christ, but do not involve the rod specifically.[242]

Paul even on one occasion used the "rod" as a symbol of judgment against the Corinthian Church.[243] This is not literal and Paul meant it symbolically which has been pointed out in other sections of this book.

The apostle Paul also refers to himself administering beatings on Christians. Prior to his conversion to Christianity, Paul mentioned that: "I was imprisoning and beating in every synagogue them who were believing on thee."[244] This shows that beatings were common punishments given to those who had committed crimes. This included Christians who were accused of

---

[242] Christ is mentioned several times as being a recipient of beating such as Mark 15:19. Paul is also "smitten on the mouth" in Acts 23:2,3
[243] I Corinthians 4:21
[244] Acts 22:19

breaking one of the Ten Commandments for believing that Jesus was divine.[245]

There are also several occasions that refer to the Apostle Paul being beaten by rods.[246] One situation refers to some public officials who had Paul and Silas beaten with rods. Paul then pointed out to these officials that they were Roman citizens.[247] When he did this, the officials realized that they had made a mistake. It was permitted, according to Roman law, for the officials to have someone beaten with rods as a form of punishment for the commission of crime in which one was found guilty. It was not the illegality of being beaten with rods that Paul was against, it was the fact that it took place without he and Silas being legally "condemned" according to that law. The officials did not follow the due process of Roman law when they beat Paul and Silas without a proper trial and giving them the opportunity to defend themselves. This is shown clearly in the actions of the officials following Paul's revelation that he and Silas were Roman citizens.[248]

The other times Paul mentions "beatings with rods" has to do with a reference in the book of II Corinthians.[249] This text refers specifically to Paul's interactions with the Roman legal system and the authorities administering that system.

One of the interesting things about the Apostle Paul is he did not object to certain types of physical beatings, even with rods. These beatings were allowed in the Roman[250] and Jewish[251] legal systems of that day. This

---

[245] Exodus 20:3

[246] Acts 16:23 in addition in Acts 16:37 Paul mentions being "beaten" referring to the earlier beating mentioned in verse 23. He also mentions that "thrice was I beaten with rods" in II Corinthians 11:25.

[247] Acts 16:37

[248] Acts 16:38-39

[249] II Corinthians 11:25

[250] For the numerous references of the Roman legal system refer to *"History of the Rod in all Countries and Ages*, 2nd. Edition, 1877)

[251] See Deuteronomy 25:2,3. See also Acts 5:40 where the Apostle Peter received a beating at the hands of the Sanhedrin, or High Council in Jerusalem (see Acts 5:34, 41)

was not always the case, however. Note that when Paul was before the High Priest and the Jewish Supreme Court, he accused the High Priest of breaking the law[252] by having him smitten on the cheek.[253] The idea of forbidding unprovoked slaps is echoed by later Rabbis. Rabbi Cohen points this out as follows: "The concept of forbidding unnecessarily severe punishment was extended by the Rabbis to include an unprovoked slap by anyone on the person of another.[254]

The Jewish legal system and Paul also had some interactions. He refers to these events in the following: "Of the Jews, five times I received forty stripes save one."[255] These events have to do with Paul being found guilty of violations of Jewish law and receiving the prescribed sentence for such violations according to the Law of Moses. This Law of Moses was (and still is) the binding religious law that all Jews of that day agreed to uphold. These events, it must be understood, were not taking place outside of clear legal frameworks because the Jewish legal system of the day was quite developed and unless clear evidence was presented, one could affect the decision of the court on the basis of providing for oneself an effective defence.

A good example of this is found in Acts 23. Paul had come to Jerusalem to visit the Apostles living there. He had been found in the Temple and had been falsely accused of bringing a non-Jew into the Temple, which was strictly forbidden according to Jewish law.[256] The Bible mentions the following: "Paul perceived that the one part were Sadducees and the other

---

[252] The law which Paul seems to be referring to here is clearly that found in the book of Exodus 21:18 which refers to one Jewish believer causing injury to another.
[253] Acts 23:2,3
[254] Rabbi Abraham Chill, *The Mitzvot: The Commandments and their Rationale*, (Keter: Jerusalem, 1974), pg.483.
[255] II Corinthians 11:24
[256] Acts 21:28,29 and Acts 24:6. These texts show that this was the charge brought against Paul that he attempted to bring a non-Jew into the Temple that was legally forbidden.

part were Pharisees, he cried out in the Sanhedrin, Men and brethren, I am a Pharisee, son of Pharisees; I am being judged for the hope of the resurrection of the dead. And when he had said this, a dissension arose between the Pharisees and the Sadducees; and the multitude was divided."[257]

The important thing to remember about these "beatings" that Paul received is that these events did not take place haphazardly or without a due process taking place. Paul was an expert at Jewish Law and he used it to his advantage to avoid prosecution and that is what this text is showing. The Apostle Paul was professional lawyer of the highest calibre and he was recognized by his peers as being such.

Jesus and the act of driving out the moneychangers

Some Christians are quick to point to the example of Jesus when he went to the temple in Jerusalem at the Passover season mentioned in the Gospel of John[258] as Jesus' endorsement of bodily punishment. At that time, Jesus responded to the scene of rampant commercialism that had taken over the Temple area. In response to this scene, Jesus made "a scourge of cords."[259] This scourge of cords was not, as the context clearly shows, designed to be used on people. The Bible indicates that "he [Jesus] made a scourge of cords, and cast all out of the temple, both *the sheep and the oxen*."[260] He then "poured out the money of the changers, and overthrew their tables; and to the dove sellers he said; 'Take these hence; make not the house of my Father a house of merchandise.'"[261]

The strong indication we get from this story was that the scourge of cords was directed at the animals, not the people. There is little evidence here that Jesus used the scourge to hit the people. In fact, it is quite possible that according to the Law of Moses, it would have been forbidden for Jesus to do

---

[257] Acts 23:6-8
[258] John 2:13-17
[259] John 2:15
[260] ibid.
[261] John 2:16

so. This is because according to the Law of Moses, it is forbidden for one Jew to strike another outside of the legally sanctioned environment of the court of justice.[262] Had Jesus struck one of the people with the scourge, he could have been convicted of a crime at that time on the basis of the above-mentioned law. Those who are quick to point to this as evidence for Jesus' approval of bodily punishment may need to reconsider this position in light of the laws that governed the actions of the Jewish people at that time. People could not just go around beating other citizens. Such behaviour was illegal at that time as it is now.

Conclusion

To conclude this discussion, the data are clear. While the New Testament has numerous references to people being beaten in judicial and extra judicial circumstances, there is one thing that is absolutely clear. The events that describe beatings being administered to a circumstance took place in legally sanctioned venues such as courts.

Additionally and most importantly, while beatings are indeed discussed with a fair amount of frequency, there is not one specific reference to an incident where a parent specifically is described as administering a smacking or a beating to a child anywhere in the New Testament. On the contrary, all of the times that we do see these events described, they universally refer to interactions between and among grown adult people. To ignore this evidence in discussing this subject misses an opportunity to place the whole question of smacking into its proper context, which is outside of the culture of Christianity.

---

[262] Exodus 21:18

7

Will a smacking save your child from going to Hell?

The thought of eternal punishment is an extremely frightening idea. The idea that people will be eternally separated from God and will suffer in an ever burning hell fire has to be one of the scariest thoughts that the imagination can conjure up. One cannot think of a more frightening thing. It is safe to say that if one knew that one could guarantee one's children a place in heaven, one would be willing to do almost anything.[263] This especially is the case when one thinks that one's actions could have some influence in saving their children from the fate of eternal punishment. This idea creates a huge sense of responsibility that has been placed upon the parent.

Among numerous Christian groups, a teaching has emerged that smacking your children is not only capable of saving them from an eternity in Hell, but smacking is the central means to see that this never takes place. Because of this teaching, numerous Christian teachers have whole-heartedly advocated for smacking children from the earliest of ages to save them from going to Hell.

Where did this responsibility have its origin? It is found in one Biblical verse that is the sole source for this concept. There is no doubt that on the basis, primarily, of this one verse, many thousands of Christian parents have lived lives of supreme pain and immense suffering over their wayward

---

[263] This would include administering a smacking.

children and the thought that their children will be assigned a place in eternal torment. This is no doubt true, but how does this Biblical verse stand up to the scrutiny of an academic examination?

In this chapter we are going to look at this verse under the microscope. The microscope we will use will be a simple but thorough examination of the Bible to better understand this verse and what it means. We'll also consider the comments of some learned scholars to help us understand what this verse means. Before we begin, let us first look at the Biblical verse in question. It is found in the book of Proverbs and it directly relates the idea of smacking children with their eternal destination. It reads as follows: "Do not withhold correction from the child: for if thou beatest him with the rod, he shall not die. Thou shalt beat him with the rod, and deliver his soul from hell.[264]

Let me say from the beginning, that I believe this Scripture to be true if we interpret it correctly. This, however, is where the problem comes in and the problem really finds its origin primarily in one word in the verse. It is the use of the word "Hell." (There is a second word that relates to this first word "Hell" that influences this interpretation in this verse and we shall deal with it shortly.)

It is the use of this word "Hell" in this verse that Christian smacking advocates have taken literally and they have created the doctrine that a smacking can save your child from going to Hell. It is this precise meaning that many influential conservative Christian groups, prominent Christian psychologists and Bible teachers assign to this verse. For example, one prominent Christian teacher refers to this idea by saying: "God has ordained issues of the greatest importance to hinge upon the discipline of the rod – even involving the child's eternal salvation."[265] Another modern pastor says the following: "The parent who spanks the child keeps him from going to

---

[264] Proverbs 23:13-14 quoted from the King James Version
[265] Larry Christenson, *The Christian Family*, pg. 112

hell. ... The parent has kept his child from hell by teaching him truths that can be learned only by discipline and the use of the rod."[266]

Modern Bible interpreters are not alone in their understanding of this verse. We find that many influential conservative Protestant theologians since the time of the Protestant Reformation have embraced this idea.[267] An example of this idea is referred to in the following quote: "The gentle rod of the mother is a very soft and gentle thing: it will break neither bone nor skin; yet by the blessing of God with it, and upon wise application of it, it would break the bond that bindeth up corruption in the heart ... Withhold not correction from the child, for it thou beatest him with the rod he shall not die, that shalt beat him with the rod and deliver his soul from hell."[268]

I believe that all of these individuals quoting this passage and interpreting it in the way that they are doing it are deeply sincere Christian people. It is not their sincerity or commitment to God, however, that needs questioning here. It is the interpretation of this verse.

Does this verse really mean that by smacking your children, you will save them from the eternity of an ever-burning hell fire? It seems a sensible approach to look at this matter of such importance carefully and truly examine what the Bible means.

To begin, let us look behind the English word "hell" in Proverbs 23:13-14 to the Hebrew original. The entire book of Proverbs was written in ancient Hebrew and it is this language that is translated into English in our modern Bibles. Now what is the word that is translated "*hell*" in this verse from Proverbs? It is the Hebrew word "*sh'ol*." It is often transliterated in English as "*sheol*," but the "e" is not found in the Hebrew original, so I have not included it here. Now, this word is translated as "*hell*" 28 times in the

---

[266] Rev. Jack Hyles, *How to Rear Children*, pgs.95-96
[267] Numerous quotes are given in this regard in Philip Greven's book, "*Spare the Child:...*" and in Alice Miller's book, "*For Your Own Good.*"
[268] John Eliot, *The Harmony of the Gospel*, Quoted in A. Miller's "*For Your Own Good,*" Intro. pg. xx

Hebrew Bible (the Old Testament).[269] This, however, is not the most interesting thing about this word. This word, *"sh'ol"* is found 65 times in the Hebrew Bible.[270] So we have 37 instances in the Hebrew Bible where this word *"sh'ol"* is translated by another word, not by the English word *"hell."* This is significant. Could it be that this word *"sh'ol"* in Hebrew does not specifically refer exactly to the common concept of *hell?*

Now, one would think that when one is talking about the concept of *"hell"* in the Bible, we are dealing with a very clear and straightforward idea. Hell is a place of burning fire and it is where sinners go to burn there forever. There is no way to get out once you go there and you stay there forever. Now this is your standard definition of *"hell."* With this in mind, now, let us look at the use of this word *"sh'ol"* in the Bible to see how this word relates to the standard definition of *"hell."*

The use of *"sh'ol"* in the Bible

The first time we encounter the use of the word *"sh'ol"* is in the book of Genesis. The story in question concerns the response of the patriarch Jacob who was told that his son, Joseph, had been killed. Let us look at this text. The Bible says the following: "And Jacob rent his clothes, and put sackcloth on his loins, and mourned for his son many days. And all his sons and all his daughters rose up to comfort him; but he refused to be comforted; and he said, For I will go down to my son mourning into the *grave*. Thus his father wept for him."[271]

Now I said that this word *"sh'ol"* appears in this verse in the book of Genesis? It is the italicised word mentioned just near the end of the verse. It is the word *"grave."* From this verse, we see that the patriarch Jacob believed that he, himself, would "go down to my son mourning into the grave."

---

[269] WEHCC, pg. 1220, under section *"sh'ohl"*
[270] ibid., Please refer to appendix 1: "The Biblical uses of the word *"sh'ol"* and the variances in English translation found in the King James Version."
[271] Genesis 37:35

(Hebrew: *sh'ol*) Based upon what Jacob said, he clearly believed that his son Joseph was now in "the grave." (Hebrew: *sh'ol*) This is a fact that is not disputed. Now, I think that any objective person examining this text would agree that Jacob and Joseph are not presently burning in "*hell*" on the basis of this verse? The text does not indicate this. However, it must be understood that the word here translated "*grave*" and the word translated "*hell*" in Proverbs 23:13-14 are exactly the same word in the original Hebrew language. Now how is it that the word "*grave*" and the word "*hell*" are translated by the same word from the Hebrew language? Before we answer this question let us look at some more examples of the use of this word "*sh'ol*."

One of the most interesting texts concerning the use of this word "*sh'ol*" concerns that surrounding an incident in the life of Jonah the prophet. Most people are fairly familiar with the story of Jonah. A fish swallowed him. Now while in the belly of the fish, Jonah said the following: "Then Jonah prayed unto the LORD his God out of the fish's belly, and said, I cried by reason of mine affliction unto the LORD, and He heard me; out of the belly of hell (Hebrew: *sh'ol*) cried I, and thou heardest my voice."[272] This is the exact same word that Jacob spoke of as "the grave." Here Jonah calls it "*hell*." He clearly is referring to the belly of the fish as a type of "*hell*" because this location is nowhere near the traditional description of hell because Jonah returned from it after leaving the belly of the fish. He did not spend eternity there, so this usage does not refer to an eternal state.

This word "*sh'ol*" is also translated by another word in English. It is the word "*pit*." We find this taking place in only three verses. Two times this takes place in the following quotation: "But if the LORD make a new thing, and the earth open her mouth, and swallow them up, with all that appertain unto them, and they go down quick into the pit (Hebrew: *sh'ol*); then ye shall understand that these men have provoked the LORD. And it came to pass,

---

[272] Jonah 2:1-2

as he had made an end of speaking all the these words, that the ground clave asunder that was under them: And the earth opened her mouth, and swallowed them up, and their houses, and all the men that appertained unto Korah, and all their goods. They, and all that appertained to them, went down alive into the pit (Hebrew: *sh'ol*), and the earth closed upon them: and they perished from among the congregation."[273] Now, clearly the verse shows that the people lost their lives, but this idea doesn't really seem to relate to the traditional teaching of "hell." The text doesn't mention anything about them remaining there for eternity. It just says that the people went down "alive into the pit." The point with this whole discussion is that the Biblical meaning of the word "*sh'ol*" is not universally an ever-burning hell fire.

To make the matter even more confusing, we not only find the word "*sh'ol*" translated as "hell," "pit," and "grave," but it is also translated by two of these words in one single verse! The following quote is one of the most interesting of this group of verses that actually features this word "*sh'ol*" several times. It comes from the book of Job.

Let us look at it here: "If I wait, the grave (Hebrew: *sh'ol*) is mine house: I have made my bed in the darkness. I have said to corruption, Thou art my father: to the worm, Thou art my mother, and my sister. And where is now my hope? As for my hope, who shall see it? They shall go down to the bars of the pit (Hebrew: *sh'ol*), when our rest together is in the dust."[274]

In this verse, we find the same word in Hebrew (*sh'ol*) translated by two different English words. They are "grave" and "pit." If you look at the context of this verse, Job is clearly speaking about the day he will die and will go and meet his family who had already died. They would one day be in the same place "when our rest together is in the dust."[275] Clearly, this verse in no way points to a traditional conception of hell at all. This is the reason why the translators of the King James Version did not place the word "hell" for

---

[273] Numbers 16:30-33
[274] Job 17:13-16 King James Version
[275] Job 17:16

the word "*sh'ol*" in this verse. Clearly, Job identified "*sh'ol*" with the resting place of the dead. Additionally, in one Bible version, the word translated as "corruption" in the above verses is also translated by the word "pit" as well.[276] Now this just adds to the confusion.

The point in this whole discussion is that this word translated as "hell" clearly does not always mean an ever-burning hell fire. This is what the great Christian theologian and scholar H.A. Ironside pointed out in his commentary on the book of Proverbs. Commenting on this specific verse in question, he said: "Sheol is not exactly hell. It is the world of the spirits."[277] Another prominent Christian commentator on the book of Proverbs refers to this passage and specifically avoids that use of the word hell in this verse.

Note the following: "Thou shalt beat him with the rod, and shalt deliver his soul from Sheol."[278] Dr. Randall Heskett, Professor of Old Testament at the Toronto School of Theology in his excellent article titled: Proverbs 23:13-14 also specifically avoids translating this word "*sh'ol*" as "hell."[279] This is where the problem comes in saying that in Proverbs 23:13-14 the word "*sh'ol*" means an ever burning hell fire. There is no clear justification for this interpretation outside of looking at the King James Version translation and simply just saying that is what it means. The Biblical information regarding this word simply won't support this thesis.

Now how does this information affect the meaning of the book of Proverbs? Can't we know it really does mean "hell" because it says "and shalt deliver his soul from hell."[280] Because the verse speaks about the word "soul" (Hebrew: *nephesh*), doesn't this show that this verse is speaking about the child's eternal soul? If so then it must be talking about "hell"? The only

---

[276] The Jerusalem Bible, Koren Edition, pg. 838
[277] H.A. Ironside, *Notes of the Book of Proverbs*, pg.323, Loizeaux Brothers, Bible Truth Depot: 1907.
[278] Tyndale Old Testament Commentary, Proverbs, pg. 51, Inter-Varsity Press, 1964.
[279] Heskett, *Interpretation Journal*, April 2001, Pgs 183.
[280] Proverbs 23:14

problem with this suggestion is the word in the King James Version once again translated as "soul." In actual fact, this word does not always mean an eternal soul! In actual fact, this word, on many occasions, does not even refer to human beings! This is an absolute fact. Let us consider this information because it bears directly on this discussion.

One of the most interesting things about the usages of this word "soul" (Hebrew: *nephesh*) is that on the first usage of it in the Bible, it doesn't even refer to a human being at all. Look at the following from the first chapter of the book of Genesis: "And God said, Let the waters bring forth abundantly the moving creature (Hebrew: *nephesh*) that hath life, and fowl that may fly above the earth in the open firmament of heaven."[281] What we find in this verse is that the Hebrew word translated "soul" in Proverbs 23:14 is in this verse translated "creature." The context clearly refers to animals. Note later we find that "the Lord God formed man of the dust of the ground, and breathed into his nostrils the breath of life; and man became a living soul (Hebrew: *nephesh*)."[282] So we have the same word referring to a human and to animals.[283] This doesn't bode well for the idea that the Hebrew word "*nephesh*" always refers to the eternal soul because there are numerous cases in the Hebrew Bible where it does not.

Not only does this same word refer to humans singularly, it refers to them collectively. Note the following: "And all the souls that came out of the loins of Jacob were seventy souls."[284] In this context, this word does not in any way refer to the eternal soul idea.

In summary, what we find in the King James Version, which has influenced most English versions profoundly, are 49 different words or

---

[281] Genesis 1:20
[282] Genesis 2:7
[283] See also Leviticus 24:17 and 24:18. One of these verses speaks about killing a man and another speaks about killing an animal, but the same Hebrew word (*nephesh*) is used.
[284] Exodus 1:5

phrases translated from the Hebrew word *"nephesh."*[285] This creates a very difficult problem for the average Bible student attempting to decipher the actual meaning of the Bible. There is no justification for this on the part of the people who translated the King James Version, but it makes sense considering a committee of 54 different men did the work. Obviously one person thought a word meant one thing and another thought it meant another, but to have 49 different words for the same word in Hebrew is problematic when it comes to developing a coherent understanding of the word from the original languages.

This fact also applies to the word *"sh'ol"* and it accounts for the reason why we find different English words relating back to a single Hebrew word. There is no need to do this, however, unless the Hebrew text by the context given gives us a compelling reason to follow this tact. In the vast majority of situations, this approach is simply unnecessary.

The modern beginning of the problem:
The King James Version

How is it that the word *"grave"* and the word *"hell"* are translated by the same word from the Hebrew language? When English Bible versions began to appear, the people who constructed these Bibles were often made up of committees who did the work of translating the Bible. The King James Version was such a production. The King James Version, which was produced in 1611, became the most influential English version for the next three hundred years. The scholars who translated the King James Version were 54 in number and sometimes they used different words in English to explain what the Hebrew words meant. Sometimes, this did not work out well. This is such a case of that phenomenon.

---

[285] WEHCC, pg, 1416

What this information shows is that the interpretation that children who are not spanked are in danger of going to Hell just won't stand up to serious textual examination. While it might be pointed out that early Hebrews believed that physical punishment was suitable for certain people of a certain age after everything else had failed within the environment of the Law of Moses (as I have pointed out in other sections of this volume), the indication from the text seems strongly to point to getting the wayward person back on the straight and narrow way so that they would save their being from dying later in life due to a criminal life or bad habits. It doesn't say when or for how long. It just says to save them from the grave. Obviously, this is good advice, and early Jews believed in corporal punishment as a very last resort for those who had moved into a position of breaking law, but to say that this verse specifically refers to eternal punishment is simply reading an interpretation into the text that the Biblical evidence will not allow.

8

"Chasten thy son while there is hope, and let not thy soul spare for his crying"

In the last chapter, we discussed the subject of the use of the word *"sh'ol"* in Proverbs 23:13-14 and the problems associated with the interpretation that is applied to this verse by many religious teachers who are advocating smacking. This verse in Proverbs 23:13-14 is not the only verse relating to smacking, however, that poses some serious problems when we look at the actual meaning in the original languages. Another key verse along this same line is found in Proverbs 19:18 and is the title for this chapter. Let us look at it. It says: "Chasten thy son while there is hope, and let not thy soul spare for his crying."[286]

On the basis of this verse cited above, numerous advocates of smacking have developed complex doctrines concerning the need for children to cry during and after being spanked. For example, one pastor in his book on child rearing points out that: "The smacking should be administered firmly. It should be painful and it should last until the child's will is broken. It should last until the child is *crying*, not tears of anger but tears of a broken will.[287] Another author follows the same line of thinking: "After correction, a parent needs to allow a child to cry for a reasonably short amount of time. Then a child should be told to stop *crying* and be brought

---

[286] Proverbs 19:18 King James Version

[287] Jack Hyles, *How to Rear Children* (Hammond, Ind.: Hyles-Anderson Publishers, 1972), pp.99-100

under control."[288] Probably one of the most prominent religious advocates of smacking children puts the same thought this way. He says: "Real *crying* usually lasts two minutes or less, but may continue for five. After that point, the child is merely complaining, and the change can be recognized in the tone and intensity of his voice. I would require him to stop the protest crying, usually by offering him a little more of what caused the original tears."[289]

There is one theme that is common throughout the last three quotes that I have given above. It is the word "*crying*." These advocates of smacking, by using this word, are specifically referring to this passage in the book of Proverbs as their justification for this suggestion. There can be no doubt that this is the case. They are not alone in suggesting this idea. Thousands of pastors and Bible teachers suggest exactly the same thing on the basis of using this single verse as their Biblical authority. There is, however, a problem with this whole idea. Let us look at this verse in Proverbs 19 in greater detail. Before we do that, however, let us place the question of "crying" as it is laid out in the book of Proverbs as a whole in context.

The use of the word "*crying*" in the book of Proverbs

The book of Proverbs mentions the concept of "*crying*" on 10 different occasions. Let us look at these individually. First, we find the three usages of the Hebrew word "*rah-nan.*" These are as follows and the corresponding English word is italicised in these texts: "Wisdom *crieth* without; she uttereth her voice in the streets."[290] Next, note the next usage: "She[291] *crieth* at the gates..."[292] Finally, the last usage of this word in Proverbs: "In the

---

[288] Roy Lessin, *Smacking: Why When How?* (Minneapolis: Bethany House Publishers, 1979), pg.79
[289] Dr. James Dobson, *Dare to Discipline* (Wheaton, Ill.: Tyndale House; & Glendale, Calif.: Regal House, 1970), pg.13
[290] Proverbs 1:20 King James Version
[291] Referring her again to the subject of "Wisdom" who is the speaker in a great part of the Proverbs 1-9.
[292] Proverbs 8:3 King James Version

transgression of an evil man there is a snare: but the righteous doth *sing* and rejoice."[293]

What we find in these contexts (and the others featuring this word Hebrew "*rah-nan)*," is that this word is most often translated into English by the words "*sing*," "*shout*," "*sang*," "*cry out*," *rejoice*," "*shout aloud for joy*," "*triumph*," and "*shouteth*."[294] At no time in any text, neither in Proverbs, nor any other Biblical book where this word is used, does this word ever refer to crying in the sense of tears, either of joy or pain.

Next, we find four instances where the concept of "*crying*" is again mentioned in Proverbs. This concerns the use of the Hebrew word "*hah-mah*." Let us look at them now. First, we have the following: "She *crieth* in the chief place of concourse, in the openings of the gates:"[295] Next, we have two texts speaking of impious women: "She is *loud* and stubborn; her feet abide not in her house."[296] We also have the following: "A foolish woman is *clamorous*; she is simple, and knoweth nothing."[297] Finally, note this text: "Wine is a mocker, strong drink is *raging*..."[298] Now what is interesting about these four texts is that while the original word in Hebrew "*hah-mah*" is translated by four different words in English that are italicised in the texts above (crieth, loud, clamorous and raging), none of these words or texts relate to the idea of "*crying*" which brings tears.

We also have two other examples of "*crying*" found in Proverbs. They are found in the following text. "Whoso stoppeth his ears at the *cry* of the poor, he also shall *cry* himself, but shall not be heard."[299] The first word translated "*cry*" is in Hebrew "*z-gah-kah*." This word does occasionally refer to crying, even of children.[300] The second word translated "*cry*" is the Hebrew

---

[293] Proverbs 29:6 King James Version
[294] Wigram's Hebrew and Chaldee Concordance, pg. 1177
[295] Proverbs 1:21 King James Version
[296] Proverbs 7:11 King James Version
[297] Proverbs 9:13 King James Version
[298] Proverbs 20:1 King James Version
[299] Proverbs 21:13 King James Version
[300] See Jeremiah 48:4

word "*gah-nah*." This word is translated numerous ways in the Hebrew Bible, but never in the sense of "*crying*" with tears.[301]

So we are left with one final verse that refers to "*crying*" and it is the verse that this chapter is named after. It is Proverbs 19:18. Let us look at it once again. "Chasten thy son while there is hope, and let not thy soul spare for his *crying*." Once again, I have italicised the word "*crying*" in the King James Version and it is this verse that, as I said previously, provides the justification for smacking proponents to strongly recommend that children who are spanked be brought to the state of crying with tears.

There is only one problem with this interpretation. It doesn't hold up to even the most simple of examinations of the meaning of the Hebrew words.

The word translated "*crying*" in Proverbs 19:18 is the Hebrew word "*mooth*." This word is used well over 500 times in the Hebrew Bible and is translated by about 40 different cognate words that all refer and are translated by words relating, without ambiguity or exception (except for this single verse we are here discussing) to the concept of death! Only in this verse did the King James Version translators render this word by the English word "*crying*."

This word has nothing even remotely related to crying that brings tears at all. What we have here is a very bad mistranslation.[302]

Modern Bible scholars recognize this fact almost universally.[303] First, the Revised Standard Version, in reference to this verse says: "do not set your heart on his destruction.[304] J. B Rotherman's excellent translation renders it as follows: "Correct thy son, because there is hope, Yet not so as to slay him …"[305] Finally, in the Interlinear Bible, we have the following: "Chasten your

---

[301] Wigram's Hebrew and Chaldee Concordance, pgs. 962-5
[302] See Wigram's Hebrew and Chaldee Concordance, pgs. 675-681
[303] Note that some scholars have suggested that this verse refers back to the verb in Hebrew "hah-mah" and could therefore be rendered "his anguish" or "his crying," but this opinion is held by a small minority of scholars.
[304] The Interpreters Bible (Nashville.: Abingdon Press), pg. 894
[305] The Emphasized Bible (Fleming Revell, 1902), Proverbs 19:18, pg. 624

son while there is hope; and do not set your soul on making him die."[306] By correcting the translation, a whole different meaning to the verse arises. The feeling shifts away from harsh, legalistic judgment to one of moderation. It shows that there are actions that parents can and should take to correct behaviour of a wayward child. [within the environment of the Law of Moses as pointed out before.] However, these actions should not be taken to extremes. This is clearly implied by the meaning of this verse. This verse could be argued to be against aggressive forms of punishment.

When we look at this verse, the use of the word "hope" is most important. We get a strong indication that the latter portion of the verse points to a situation where hope is now lost. This is certainly in evidence if an uncorrected life leads one down the path of crime, which in the Mosiac system could lead to the death penalty. This seems a much more clear interpretation based upon the context and it is this idea that most Christian authorities assign to this verse. Certainly, no parent would lose hope in a child due to his crying, but one certainly would find oneself in a hopeless situation if his or her child were moving down the path towards death.

Additionally, we find that while there are over 20 Hebrew words that relate to "*crying out*," "*crying aloud*," "*to cry*", etc. not one of these words is found in the whole book of Proverbs.[307]

Not only that, there are six different Hebrew words that refer to the concept of "*weeping*" which involves tears on numerous occasions. In actual fact, a careful examination of these words will show that they rarely refer to children. One example where one of them does refer to a child concerns the discovery of the baby Moses by Pharaoh's daughter. The text says: "And when she had opened it (the box in which Moses lay), she saw the child: and, behold, a weeping boy."[308] More often though you find these words describing weeping having to do with people weeping over the deaths of

---

[306] The Interlinear Bible (Peabody.: Hendrickson), Proverbs 19:18, pg.522
[307] See Wigram's Hebrew and Chaldee Concordance, pg. 1503
[308] Exodus 2:6

loved ones, over deaths in battle, over deaths of holy men or kings and similar situations.[309] The important thing to point out in this context, however, is that these words are conspicuous in the book of Proverbs: conspicuous for their absence![310] These six Hebrew words translated by *"weeping,"* *"wept"* and *'weep"* are not found once in Proverbs.

Finally, there is only one word in the Bible that is translated and means exactly without exception "tears." This is the Hebrew word *"dim-gah."* This word means *"tears"* (as a result from crying or weeping) exactly and this word also does not appear in the whole book of Proverbs even one time.[311]

In summary, looking at the evidence as a whole, the concepts of *"crying," "weeping"* and *"tears"* are not discussed within the pages of the book of Proverbs. Based on this evidence, the idea that the Biblical book of Proverbs advises parents or any other person to spank children to induce crying and bring forth tears is without any foundation or basis according to the data found in the Biblical texts.

---

[309] Wigram's Hebrew and Chaldee Concordance, pg. 1672
[310] ibid., pg. 1672
[311] ibid., pg.346

9

A rod is for the back or the buttocks?

One of the most problematic teachings promoted by religious advocates of smacking children is the almost universal opinion that children, who are to be spanked, are to receive the smacking on the buttocks. The problem with this teaching comes to light with a very simple examination of the Biblical passages that are used as proof for the necessity of this practice.

A good example of this is found in the following quote from a smacking advocate. "God has given the parents the perfect area on which to administer a smacking – the child's bottom."[312] Another smacking proponent points out that "God, in His wisdom, prepared a strategic place on your children's anatomy which has enough cushiony, fatty tissue and sensitive nerve endings to respond to Spirit-led stimulation. This area is the base of the back, above the thighs, located on the backside of every child."[313]

It is clear from these quotes that these proponents of smacking have certain Biblical passages in mind to support these positions. The Biblical references in question are the following:

"In the lips of him that hath understanding wisdom is found: but a rod is for the back of him that is void of understanding."[314]

---

[312] Roy Lessin, *Smacking: Why When How?* (Minneapolis: Bethany House Publishers, 1979), pg. 74-75
[313] Larry Tomczak, *God, the Rod and Your Child's Bod*, pg. 118.
[314] Proverbs 10:13 (King James Version)

"Judgment are prepared for scorners, and stripes for the *back* of fools."[315]

"A whip for the horse, a bridle for the ass, a rod for the fool's *back*."[316]

Note: It is interesting, in this context, that the phrase "son" or "father" is not mentioned, but rather these texts seem to address "fools" or "those lacking understanding."

Some Christian teachers point out that the Bible indicates that the rod was to be used on the back, but then give a preference for the buttocks in the same context. A good example of this is found in the following quote: "The rod should be used on the bare back, preferably on the buttocks, especially on younger children."[317]

There is only one simple question that arises from this matter. If the Bible meant the rod should be applied to the buttocks, why does the Bible say "the back?" This is an important question that needs answering by smacking advocates because we find a perfectly clear Hebrew word in the Bible translated "buttocks" and that is exactly what the word means. Note the following texts that show the usages of this word.

The prophet Isaiah was commanded by God to do the following. "In the year that Tartan came unto Ashdod (when Sargon the King of Assyria sent him) and fought against Ashdod, and took it; at the same time spake the LORD to Isaiah the son of Amoz, saying: 'Go and loose the sackcloth from off thy loins, and put off thy shoe from thy foot.' And he did so walking naked and barefoot. And the LORD said, "Like my servant Isaiah hath walked naked and barefoot three years for a sign and wonder upon Egypt and upon Ethiopia, so shall the King of Assyria lead away the Egyptians

---

[315] Proverbs 19:29 (King James Version)
[316] Proverbs 26:3 (King James Version)
[317] J.R. Fugate, *What the Bible says about Child Training* (Garland, Texas: Alethia Publishers, 1980, pg. 143.

prisoners, and the Ethiopians captives, young and old, naked and barefoot, even with their *buttocks* uncovered, to the shame of Egypt."[318]

Some might say that this text doesn't really mean "naked" completely, yet the Hebrew word used for the word "naked" (Hebrew: *ghah-rohm*) is the exact same word used in the book of Genesis to describe the bodily condition of Adam and Eve prior to the time they clothed themselves.[319] The patriarch Job also used this word when saying: "Naked came I out of my mother's womb, ..."[320]

In this context of Isaiah 20, note the phrase "with their buttocks uncovered."[321] This Hebrew word for buttocks (*shehth*) means buttocks in the sense that people today refer to the buttocks area. This is defined further in another Biblical verse. Note the following text referring to an event in King David's time. King David sent emissaries to a neighbouring country who was previously David's ally. These emissaries of David were not received very well. "Wherefore Hanun took David's servants, and shaved off the one half of their beards, and cut off their garments in the middle, even to their *buttocks*, and sent them away."[322]

The first thing to note concerns the garments these men were wearing. As Jews adhering to the law of Moses, they would have been wearing outer garments made of a single piece of woven cloth like those demanded in the Law of Moses for adherents to Judaism.[323] These garments were made from a single piece of cloth. There was a hole in the middle of them and this is where the head of the wearer of the garment was placed. Then, the garment stretched down covering the whole body and it was uniform in length in the

---

[318] Isaiah 20:1-4 (King James Version)
[319] See Genesis 2:25; I Samuel 19:24; Job 1:21; 22:6; 24:7; 24:10; 26:6; Ecclesiastes 5:15; Isaiah 20:2; 20:3; 20:4; 58:7; Hosea 2:3; Amos 2:16 and Micah 1:8.
[320] Job 1:21
[321] Isaiah 20:4
[322] II Samuel 10:4
[323] See Numbers 15:38 and Rabbi Abraham Chill, *The Mitzvot: The Commandments and their Rationale*, Keter Books; Jerusalem, 1974, pgs. 338-341.

front and the back. Fringes (Hebrew: *tzitzit*) were placed on each corner of the garment according to the Law of Moses.[324]

As the text mentions, these garments were "cut off … in the middle, even to the buttocks."[325] If one were to cut this garment we are talking about here in the fashion mentioned in the text, the lower part of the body would be exposed leaving the upper part of the body covered. There is no doubt how David's men felt about this event taking place. "When they told it unto David, he sent to meet them, because the men were greatly ashamed …"[326] Note it is also clear from the text that the same also concerned them having their beards shaven.[327]

These texts show that the Hebrew language has a word for buttocks (*shehth*), clearly and plainly. Smacking advocates need to explain why they interpret the word "back" as "buttocks" when the Bible uses the word "back" and "buttocks" in different contexts? If the Bible means buttocks, this word is used in other contexts to mean buttocks. It is providing a seemingly personal opinion concerning this interpretation to say "back" means "buttocks."

---

[324] Numbers 15:38
[325] II Samuel 10:4
[326] ibid.
[327] ibid.

10

The theological interpretation of a smacking

This may seem an odd title for a chapter, but it is specifically titled as such to introduce a subject that needs discussion and clarification in this context. It may also seem somewhat of a complex subject only to be discussed by religious university professors at the graduate students level. However, this is not true at all. All Christian parents desire their actions to please God. This is especially the case when it comes to matters of children and how we are to raise them, care for them and guide them into adulthood.

Now, the only reason that I can see in the Bible and in all of the commentaries and books written about this subject is the fact that smackings are given as punishment. This reason is because of wrong actions. To rehearse the evidence for this fact is not needed in this context as it has been covered amply in other areas of this work. The point is, smackings are given as punishment. They are to be used as tools for punishment. Smackings are given in response to a wrong act committed by a child and are designed to show the child that he or she made a mistake (or in theological language, committed a "sin") and by giving the smacking, we then reinforce this idea in a way that will remind the child not to "sin" again.

Now, the key point that I wish to introduce here is this. Smackings only take place in an environment of law. What I mean by this is quite simple. When a parent spanks a child, a legal environment has been entered into. The parent assumes the role of judge, jury and punisher, while the child is the defendant in the case. For example, John's mother told him not to go into the kitchen because the floor was wet. John went into the kitchen despite his mother's wishes and got the floor dirty with his muddy shoes. His mother found out and pronounced him "guilty." Then she "sentenced" him to a smacking as "punishment." John received the smacking as punishment and the crime had then been paid for. John was now free to do as he wished again (within his families rules). He was no longer facing or under a punishment. This chain of events represents a simple but clear legal proceeding.

We find the same chain of events taking place in a number of Biblical examples given by the Apostle Paul that refer specifically to punishments he received and his reactions to them. Let us first look at Acts 23. This section of the Bible reveals a legal proceeding, or a court case, that took place with the Apostle Paul as the defendant. He was brought before the Sanhedrin of the Jewish people. Now, this was not any simple court. It represented the Supreme Court of the Jewish nation. It had 71 members and was a very solemn assembly. Only legal scholars of the highest calibre were allowed to be on this body.

The Apostle Paul was brought before this body accused of a crime. He was accused by the Israelites at that time of bringing a non-Jewish person into the Temple at Jerusalem, which was a crime punishable by death.[328] Now when the Apostle Paul was brought before this court, he was permitted according to the Law of Moses[329] to defend himself. He was actually required to respond to the charges against him of bringing a non-Jew into the Temple. This is exactly what he proceed to do. He first comments that he has been a faithful citizen toward God until that day. At that point, a very interesting thing took place. Paul was smitten on the mouth by an associate of the existing High Priest.[330] At that point, Paul accused the man, who he did not

---

[328] Acts 21:8. This Scripture says that the Jews of Asia accused Paul of bringing a non-Jew into the Temple that was a crime punishable by the death penalty. Such an idea is, of course, absurd considering Paul's intimate knowledge of the Law of Moses.

[329] Deuteronomy 13:15

[330] Acts 23:3

recognize to be the High Priest, of breaking the Law of Moses[331] by ordering him to be smitten in that fashion. At that point, Paul is informed that he is addressing the High Priest of the Jewish nation: "And they that stood by said 'The High Priest of God do you revile?' And Paul said: I was not aware, brethren, that he was high priest; because it is written: 'Of a ruler of your people shall you not speak injuriously.'"[332]

Now what does this have to do with a smacking? What we are witnessing here is someone being punished by hitting him in the mouth for a sin that a recognized authority administered in a legal environment. Note that Paul pointed out his error for speaking to the High Priest in the way that he did. In a sense he apologized not to the High Priest, but to God, whom the High Priest was the representative of. Paul did not bring up the fact that he was struck again. He went on with his very effective defence.

Note the chain of events. Paul was in the Temple undergoing a personal ritual. He is accused and then brought before a court of justice to answer the charges. He begins his defense and is found guilty of a sin and punished legally. He then accepts the punishment and moves on with his defense.

The point is this. This event took place in a legal environment. When someone is struck, they have been judged as guilty of a sin, they have been sentenced and they will be punished. Whether you are talking about talking back to your mother or to the High Priest of the nation of Israel, you are in a legal environment. The smacking represents the punishment phase of the legal proceeding.

Let us look at another example given by the Apostle Paul in this regard. When Paul was in Phillipi he was accused of introducing foreign and unlawful customs among the populace of the city.[333] Paul and his companion

---

[331] Specifically Leviticus 19:15 that says that it is illegal to commit unrighteousness on someone while undergoing judgment.
[332] Acts 23:5 which refers to Exodus 22:28
[333] Acts 16:19-23

Silas were brought before the city leaders and charges were levelled against them.[334] This was a legal proceeding. Paul and Silas were then judged, found guilty and sentenced to a beating and to being thrown in jail. This is exactly what took place.[335] Now, this again shows that the beating took place in an environment of a legal proceeding.

Finally, a closing example of this the Apostle Paul actually underwent the only legally recognized method for administering the death penalty allowed in the Law of Moses.[336] He was stoned and left for dead.[337] In actual fact, this stoning was a legally sanctioned form of punishment designed to kill the criminal. This stoning was legal in every way and Paul was left for dead due to it. Note that this punishment once again took place in a legal environment.

The point to this whole discussion surrounds the fact that during the time that Paul lived, he was subject to the Law of Moses which had numerous punishments, beating with rods, stoning, striking on the mouth and the like. This was the system then and was legal at the time because the Law of Moses was the legal system at that time for Jews and Israelites and anyone else who wished to embrace that faith. But is the Law of Moses valid and in force in our times today? Are we still under the Law of Moses? Are we still under any law for that matter? What about the concept of grace? How does this fit in?

What we who are Christians today have to recognize is that we are no longer under the Law of Moses or any other law other than the Law of Christ. What is that Law of Christ? It is the Gospel of the grace of God. It is

---

[334] Acts 16:20-22

[335] Acts 16:23

[336] Stoning was the pelting of stones by a mob at a person who had merited their ill will (Exodus 8:26; 17:4; II Chronicles 24:20ff; cf. Hebrews 11:37; Acts 5:26) or the infliction of the death penalty by stoning (Leviticus 20:2; Deuteronomy 13:10). The method, which an enraged crowd took of executing vengeance with the weapons lying readiest to their hand, came to be employed afterwards as a regular and legal method of inflicting the death sentence on a criminal. Stoning is the ONLY form of capital punishment recognized in the Mosaic Law (Hasting's, vol. II, pp.528,529)

[337] Acts 14:19

this grace, or unmerited favour, that is, a favour from God that we don't deserve on the basis of our works, but He gives it to us through our attachment to and identification with Jesus Christ. Is it not this message that we, as Christians, wish to communicate to our children? The concept of the grace of God cannot be communicated to children accurately by administering a smacking. Smackings are given in environments of law, not grace. Let us look at an example of this in action in the life on one of the great Christian ministers of the last century.

Rev. Dwight Moody was one of the most famous of evangelists of the late 19th century. He was a Christian scholar who knew the difference between law and grace and he applied this difference in the way he raised his children. Rev. Moody grew up in a home dominated by law. "To these whippings (from his father) Mr. Moody always referred with great approval but with delightful inconsistency never adopted the same measure in the government of his own family. In his home grace was the ruling principal, not law, and the sorest punishment of a child was the sense that the father's loving heart had been grieved by waywardness or folly."[338] Reverend Moody understood the simple difference between grace and law. He chose the clearly spelled out New Testament teaching that "you are severed from Christ, you who would be justified by law; you are fallen away from grace."[339]

The great Protestant theologian of the last century, Karl Barth, also understood grace in the same way when it came to smacking children. Barth taught the following: "'Christian exhortation as such can never point in the direction of disciplinary severity.' To raise children 'in the discipline and instruction of the Lord, excludes provoking them to the anger, resistance, and rebellion that emerges through the 'assertion of Law, or the execution of judgment.' Admonitions in the book of Proverbs not to spare the rod of correction must be transformed by the duty to know and correspond in

---

[338] Wm. Moody, *The Life of Dwight L. Moody* (New York: Fleming Revell: 1900, pg. 24

[339] Galatians 5:4

thought and deed to grace, and in that light to summon children to repentance. A mother's and father's training and advice are to be a 'joyful invitation' to their children to rejoice with them in Jesus Christ. 'To be joyful,' Barth explains, 'is to expect that life will reveal itself as God's gift of grace, that it will present and offer itself in provisional fulfilments of its meaning and intention as movement. To be joyful means to look out for opportunities for gratitude.' The work of parents is limited by time and a receding social space in which other influences on children increasingly come into play. It is limited by the fact that parents cannot relieve their sons and daughters of personal responsibility. How much more vigorously must it be said that parents may nevertheless 'give their children the opportunity to encounter the God who is present, operative and revealed in Jesus Christ, to know him and to learn to love and fear Him,' and to that extent offer them a life that is joyful."[340] Additionally, let us seek after the Spirit of God because "if you are led by the Spirit, you are not under the Law."[341]

What these quotes show is the difference between grace and law and how two Christian scholars applied these teachings to the subject of smacking. We need to let the message of grace made clear in the New Testament speak to us and let it transform us into people of joy, being thankful for everything, understanding and applying the teachings of grace and not focusing our attention of law, judgment, punishment and sin.

In closing, the theological interpretation of a smacking is that it is a punishment for the violation of law. This law can be the law of the family, the law of the city, the law of school or the law of the government. The Bible shows, however, that "you (who are Christians) are not under the law," any law except that of the Spirit. What is the teaching or fruit of the Spirit? Love, joy, peace, longsuffering, kindness, goodness, faithfulness, gentleness, self-

---

[340] William Werpehowski, essay "*Reading Karl Barth on Children*," M. Bunge, *The Child in Christian Thought*, Eerdamns: Grand Rapids: Michigan, 2001, pgs. 399-400.
[341] Galatians 5:18

control.[342] What part of a smacking brings forth the principle of Love? of joy? of peace!? of longsuffering? of kindness? of goodness? of faithfulness? of gentleness? or of self-control? The truth is there is no part of a smacking that brings forth any of these things. On the contrary, smacking is more acclimated to those concepts found in Galatians 5:19-21. Against these fruits of the Spirit there is no law[343] and in an environment where they are taught and practiced there is no need for a smacking.

---

[342] Galatians 5:23-24
[343] ibid.

Appendix One

Misunderstanding the harshness in Biblical teachings

One of the recurring themes found in many articles and books written by psychologists or those in the children's rights/human rights community against smacking concerns some statements that are found in the Bible which seem very harsh on the surface. The fact is, there are some statements that are in the Bible, when looked at on the surface, one would come away with a very harsh, cold and unfeeling approach to life advocated by the writers of the Bible.

I could give many examples, but in this regard, I am going to focus just on one. The example is from the book of Deuteronomy chapter 21:18-21. It concerns the so-called "stubborn and rebellious" son. The text reads: "If a man have a stubborn and rebellious son, which will not obey the voice of his father, or the voice of his mother, and that, when they have chastened him, will not hearken unto them: Then shall his father and his mother lay hold on him, and bring him out unto the elders of the city, and unto the gate of his place; And they shall say unto the elders of his city, This our son is stubborn and rebellious, he will not obey our voice; he is a glutton, and a drunkard. And all the men of his city shall stone him with stones, that he die: so shalt thou put evil away from among you; and all Israel shall hear, and fear."

This text seems so clear and easy to understand. It is the death penalty without exception. Speaking about the abovementioned text from the book of Deuteronomy, Dr. Philip Greven whose excellent work I have previously quoted in this volume, interpreted this text in the following way. "Other Old Testament texts lend additional support to the punishment and violence against children advocated in the name of King Solomon. ... Thus, the price for filial disobedience is death."[344] This is a common interpretation about the harshness of the legislation outlined in the book of Deuteronomy, but does it represent an accurate historical understanding of the application of the text itself?

Looking on the surface, this interpretation is exactly that related by the text itself. Moses comes across as a harsh, legalistic and brutal writer. But is this the truth? What is required of this text is some accurate interpretation. In this regard, I wish now to refer to the work of Rabbi Abraham Chill, whose excellent book has been quoted in other sections of this work. Rabbi Chill provides a thorough historical context for interpreting this text. This text cannot be interpreted without the assistance of outside authorized authorities. Rabbi Chill, who is himself a recognized authority of Jewish law, points to almost 20 different historical sources to assist him in understanding this passage.[345] It is by referring to the intellectual giants of past scholarship that we can see the depth and breadth of opinion regarding this or any Biblical text. Rabbi Chill, a giant of Biblical scholarship, would not think for one moment of referring to this text in a historical vacuum and offer a face value estimation of its meaning.

There are two points about this text and about the death penalty in general, as it was understood in the Biblical and post-Biblical period. First, the death penalty was imposed only when the Temple in Jerusalem was in existence. "Under Jewish Law capital punishment was imposed only when the Temple was still in existence, when the offerings were still brought to the altar, and when the Sanhedrin still sat in the Chamber of Hewn Stones (in

---

[344] Greven, *Sparing the Rod*, pg. 49.
[345] Chill, *The Mitzvot*, pg. 242.

the Temple).[346] This means that no matter what this text says, following the destruction of the Temple in AD 70 by the Romans, this text has never even once been applied to anyone.

Second, death sentences were not every day occurrences. We need not to rely on the images of colourful Hollywood films that perpetuate historical inaccuracies. We need to examine the historical documents to teach us what was indeed taking place based upon eyewitness testimony. Note the following: "the death sentence was imposed only after much investigation and deliberation on the part of the court of justice. The judges made every effort to avoid imposing capital punishment. Circumstantial evidence was not accepted in trials for a capital offence and once the defendant in the such a case had been acquitted, he could not be brought to trial again for the same offence, even if direct evidence had turned up in the meantime to prove his guilt."[347] It must be pointed out here that we are speaking about a Jewish cultural background. This quote refers to "judges," the Court of Justice," "defendants," and a "case." These terms must be understood as referring to courts that were in existence to adjudicate matters of law and in this case we are talking about matters of Jewish religious law. In addition, on reading this quote, some may be reminded of the concept of "double jeopardy" which is a component of our modern Western judicial systems. Jewish legal scholars have known about "double jeopardy" for over 2000 years and it was applied in ancient times.

We find other sources making even stronger cases against the death penalty. Note the following: "Should the court find that the homicide was deliberate, sentence of death was passed; but there was great reluctance to resort to capital punishment and every endeavour was made to avoid it. Indeed, it was remarked: 'A Sanhedrin[348] which executed a person once in seven years was called destructive. Rabbi Eleazar ben Azariah said, 'Once in

---

[346] Chill, *The Mitzvot*, pg. 67.

[347] ibid., pg. 67

[348] Meaning the Supreme Court of the Jewish nation.

seventy years. Rabbi Tarphon and Rabbi Akiba said, If we were members of a Sanhedrin, never would a person be put to death.'"[349] So, we see that the death penalty itself had very strict rules and regulations associated with it.

The Stubborn and Rebellious Son

Next, what constituted a "stubborn and rebellious son?" There is no age mentioned in the text, so who decides? Rabbi Chill shows that "who is considered a 'stubborn and rebellious son'? Any young man three months past bar mitzvah age..."[350] This means that this punishment was never inflicted on anyone below the age of 13 years three months. So the concept of "son" required interpretation.

This all may sound interesting, but many may say that this is still a harsh punishment even for a child who just turned thirteen? This may be but consider this. Rabbi Chill points out that the death penalty was not the first solution to a family choosing to apply this law to their child. "The first offence reported by the parents made the boy subject to flogging; if he repeated the offence and was again brought to the court by his parents he received the death penalty – execution by stoning."[351] So, we can see that ancient Israelites were not taking their children out and stoning them to death every time a boy ate too much or drank some wine. There was strict due process involved and those accused of these crimes had legal rights before the law. When you look at it, early Jews were quite familiar with the modern concepts of human and children's rights. Much of what makes up our modern body of law today in this regard was known and practiced in ancient times.

Some might say that here we begin to see the harsh nature of this law after all. Not so fast! Rabbi Chill further adds that: "At least 23 members of the Sanhedrin had to be present when such an offender was tried. Not

---

[349] Cohen, *Everyman's Talmud*, pg. 317.
[350] Chill, pg. 241
[351] ibid.

only that, if one of his parents was lame, blind or deaf, or if one of his parents was unwilling to have him brought to court, the offender was exempt from the death penalty. This meant, in effect, that the death penalty for a 'stubborn and rebellious son' was very rarely carried out."[352]

An addition, regarding this point of the 23 judges, a majority was not sufficient to convict a person in a death penalty case. The judges had to have a majority with a minimum of two votes. This shows that such a case required a great deal of deliberation to judge the defendant guilty.[353] We also find that the junior judges in such a case had to cast their votes first on the basis of their respective ages. The older judges voted last so their votes would not influence the opinion of the younger judges.[354] By digging deeper into the history surrounding this text, we dispel the false notion that the ancient Hebrews were a brutal, violent, lawless society that stoned their children for the most minor of infractions. [This information should be a wake-up call to those in the human rights community whose attacks on the Bible often focus on this and similar verses for their criticisms levelled at the Holy Scriptures.]

We also find that the child himself was not the only one on trial. The great medieval Jewish scholar Maimonides placed some of the blame for "stubborn and rebellious sons" squarely on the parents. "How does a son become 'stubborn and rebellious'? Through the fault of the parents who are too permissive and permit him to lead a life of irresponsibility."[355] Parents who did not guide their children were a part of the problem and contributed to their children becoming "stubborn and rebellious." Two giants of Jewish scholarship further echo this idea. Rabbi Moses Al Sheikh said: "He explains why the Torah insists that parents personally bring their 'stubborn and rebellious son' to the court of justice. In this manner, he says, the parents acknowledge that they are to blame for the way in which their son has turned

---

[352] ibid.
[353] ibid., pg. 105
[354] ibid.
[355] ibid.

out. No child becomes intractable from one day to the next. The process begins when the child is at a very early age when many parents, unfortunately, tend to view such behaviour as 'just a phase.' This is a mistaken notion, and the parents are now asked to face the fact that they failed their child when he was in the greatest need of their guidance."[356]

Rabbi Ibn Ezra puts it a little bit stronger placing some of the blame on the parents: "He is not prepared to place the burden of responsibility entirely on the child. The son can be justifiably tried and punished for his behaviour only if the conduct of his parents themselves has been beyond reproach. If they did not provide a good example for him to emulate, they have no right to bring him to court for 'stubborn and rebellious' conduct."[357] So what we find is that not only the son is on trial, the parents as well have to demonstrate that they did the right things. If not, no death penalty will ever be inflicted.

In closing this appendix, it has been my goal to broaden the understanding of this particular verse. I hope that this discussion has brought new perspectives to this particular verse. I hope that we will all look underneath the surface of what these texts say and get some other opinions into their meanings. By doing this, we follow the Biblical suggestion to get several witnesses in establishing a Biblical fact.[358] This is the least we can do for the next generations ahead of us.

---

[356] ibid., pg. 242
[357] ibid.
[358] II Corinthians 13:1; I Timothy 5:19.

Appendix Two

Punishment: Does it work?
A Biblical examination

What is the reason for punishment? Is it revenge? Is it retribution? Is it justice? Is it training? Is it teaching? Why do we punish children? I think that most people would say that we punish children because we want to teach them right from wrong and that by punishing them we give them an experience of what happens in life when one does wrong. But is this idea an accurate picture of what children can expect from life? How does this idea stack up to Biblical evidence? What does the Bible say about doing right and wrong? This is an important question because it bears directly on what sort of lessons we wish to impart to our children. Let us look at the Biblical examples and see how God looks at punishment.

The first example from the Bible in regarding the effectiveness of punishment concerns Noah. Prior to the judgment by water in the time of Noah, the Bible shows that God was very unhappy with the actions of people on the earth. Noah was aware of God's displeasure. The thoughts and actions of humanity at that time were only evil continually.[359] Now, God decided to put an end to all life forms on earth at that time.[360] This was a serious punishment of humanity for their sins at that time. However, there was one

---

[359] Genesis 6:5-6
[360] Genesis 6:7

small family headed by Noah that found favour in God's eyes.[361] Now, after witnessing the judgment by water that took place, by seeing the rainbow in the sky and by experiencing the divine presence of God in a special way, you would think that this would make a huge difference in the actions of Noah. You would think that seeing this divine punishment take place that it would affect Noah's behaviour? One would think that Noah would now follow a new direction for the new world? However, what took place in the life of Noah just a short time after this punishment? Noah got drunk with wine and found himself uncovered in his tent.[362] Did witnessing the judgment of water and seeing all the destruction and death that took place change the behaviour of Noah? If so, the change was only temporary.

Let's go down to the time of the Exodus of the children of Israel from the land of Egypt. Let us rehearse the story. During the time of the Exodus, the Israelites had been living in Israel for several hundred years. They had fallen into a state of slavery under the Egyptians. Now, the Bible says that the Israelites were in a state of national crisis and they cried out to God for relief from the slavery. God heard their prayer and called Moses to help them.[363]

After seeing the ten miracles in Egypt and the mighty punishment that God placed on the Egyptians and being taken out of the land by the miracle of Passover, what happened? The Israelites were taken to Mount Sinai. There they witnessed some of the most amazing and extraordinary signs from God. If the ten miracles of punishment in Egypt were not enough, the people now saw the power of God and even heard God's own voice.[364] Upon seeing these events, "all the people answered with one voice, and said, all the words which the LORD has said we will do."[365]

---

[361] Genesis 6:8
[362] Genesis 9:20-22
[363] Exodus 2-6
[364] Deuteronomy 5:4
[365] Exodus 24:3

Sounds as if they really took the lesson of this punishment and judgment of Egypt to heart? Or did they? In actual fact, no, the people rebelled against God ten different times within the first year of leaving Egypt![366] God finally got so frustrated with the whole nation that he decided to make a nation out of Moses himself and punish these rebels.[367]

But wait a minute. What about Moses himself? Even he rebelled against the command of God on one occasion that caused him not to be permitted to pass across the Jordan River into the land of Israel.[368] It is amazing to say, but these people who witnessed some of the most incredible miraculous events and divine punishments meted out were constantly referred to as a "stiff-necked people."[369] Maybe these are just a few isolated examples though?

Look at the time just following the Exodus period in the time of Joshua. During that period, there were numerous miracles,[370] but did witnessing these miracles and observing the punishment of the people of the land change the hearts of the people for good? If so, it did not last long because the nation of Israel deteriorated to such a barbaric condition that that practically no one in the whole nation knew the God of Israel at all.[371]

Look at the following quote from the Biblical book of Judges: "And it came to pass when the judge was dead, that they relapsed, and became more corrupt than their fathers, in following other gods to serve them, and to bow down to them; they omitted nothing of their practices, nor of their stubborn way."[372]

Look at another example concerning the prophets Elijah and Elisha. Elijah the prophet pronounced several judgments that punished people, but

---

[366] Numbers 14:22
[367] Exodus 32:10
[368] Deuteronomy 32:48-52
[369] Exodus 32:9; 33:3; 33:5; 34:9; Deuteronomy 9:6; 9:13; 10:16; 31:27
[370] Joshua 10:10
[371] Judges 2:10-12
[372] Judges 2:19

did these punishments change the behaviour of the people? He prayed that it would not rain.[373] He brought fire down out of heaven three times.[374] Did these punishments change people for the good? It doesn't seem so because Elijah himself following these events still felt he was the only person in the whole nation who worshipped the true God.[375]

What about his successor Elisha? He pronounced several judgments on people that others witnessed. He performed a number of punishments that were miraculous,[376] however, the thirteen kings who ruled in the northern Kingdom of Israel from the time of Elijah and Elisha until the captivity of the nation by the Assyrians (almost 200 years later) were those who did "evil in the sight of the Lord."[377] The punishments exacted by the special miraculous period of Elijah and Elisha did nothing to correct the nation from the errors of their ways. Indeed, they got worse, and were led into captivity!

What these texts point out is a pattern. The pattern is this: God tells man not to do something. Man proceeds to break God's law and commit sin, God forgives and man is restored into unity with God. It seems that no matter what God does, man ignores Him and just goes his own way.

So, what we can see is that punishment did not work. It did not bring about a change in behaviour. It did not bring repentance.

It is not only the case that man does not respond to punishment to build righteousness and character, he does not respond to blessings either. In this regard, let me give just two examples. The first one is from the Old Testament. It concerns King Solomon.

---

[373] I Kings 17:1
[374] I Kings 18:38; II Kings 1:10 and I Kings 1:12
[375] I Kings 19:14
[376] II Kings 2:24; 5:17; 6:18
[377] This phrase is used seven times to describe the actions of the children of Israel in this period. This period is called the period of the "Judges." These "Judges" were sent by God to "reform" the people and bring them back into a close relationship with God. Read this book of the Judges and ask yourself if their actions helped reform the people at all? See Judges 2:11; 3:7; 3:12; 4:1; 6:1; 10:6; 13:1

King Solomon was one of the most blessed figures in the Bible. He was given "wisdom and largeness of heart, like the sand that is on the seashore."[378] God gave Solomon peace,[379] unimaginable wealth,[380] abundant food,[381] prestige,[382] a long life,[383] beautiful women of almost unimaginable numbers,[384] miraculous confirmations of God's presence in his life,[385] yet after seeing the life of his father and what happened to King David as well, King Solomon still disobeyed God by marrying inappropriately and worshipping his wives god's in a variety of ways.[386]

Now how did Solomon respond to these immense blessings? One would think that he would have been one of the most righteous, God fearing holy men who ever lived, but however, this is not the case at all. Solomon, after seeing all the blessings, wealth, happiness, bounty, peace and wisdom, "did evil in the sight of the Lord, and went not fully after the Lord, as did David his father."[387] God characterized Rehoboam, Solomon's son as one that did "more evil than all that were before you."[388] Now this is from the Old Testament, but the New Testament gives the same teaching. Let us consider one example.

The New Testament records a number of examples of people who saw the work of God in action. They saw incredible miracles performed by Jesus. They saw him forgiving people for their actions and saw people

---

[378] I Kings 5:9
[379] I Kings 5:5
[380] II Chronicles 1:15
[381] I Kings 5:2-3
[382] I Kings 10 which shows his interaction with numerous foreign dignitaries.
[383] Ecclesiastes 12:2-5 generally attributed to Solomon gives the appraisal of growing old. Solomon is also called "old" in I Kings 11:4. Solomon was born to David and Bathsheba after David became king in Jerusalem (II Samuel 4:5). His reign in Jerusalem encompassed 33 years. If you read the account of Solomon taking power, these are not the actions of a teenager. He must have been in his twenties (I Kings 1-2:13)
[384] I Kings 11:4
[385] II Chronicles 7:1 records the fire of God coming down from heaven.
[386] I Kings 11:1-14
[387] I Kings 11:6
[388] I Kings 13:9

supposedly changing their lives. But what did they themselves do? Look at the actions of Saint Peter. Here is someone who lived with Christ over a period of several years. He even promised on one occasion to Jesus: "Lord, with you I am ready to both to prison and to death.[389] Jesus then told him: "I tell you, Peter, the rooster shall not crow today, until you have three times denied knowing me."[390] Then what happened? Read Luke 22:55-63 for the answer.

It is absolutely amazing that after seeing all of the incredible healings and watching Christ work miracles and that Peter and bestowing blessing after blessing on others that Peter was so quick to deny Christ.

There is a point in all of these examples. The point is this. Not only do punishments not work to bring about righteous behaviour, but also blessings and miracles do not bring about righteous behaviour either. This is an especially important lesson for parents to learn when it comes to children. Now, the real question that really begs asking is if adults who saw and experienced God in a direct way were sinful and required forgiveness, what about children who do not have any real experience and are relying on us for guidance, how are we to treat them?

Engendering Righteousness: The Biblical Standard

I want to point out one example from the Bible that parents can translate well to child rearing. It has to do with learning by example. It concerns the example set by the greatest prophet in the whole Bible, John the Baptist.[391] He began his ministry in the wilderness of Judea about 25 miles east of Jerusalem. This region is one of the hottest and most inhospitable on earth, especially in the summer, yet this is where John the Baptist was teaching. He also did not live a life of luxury. He practiced what he preached and people knew it.

---

[389] Luke 22:33
[390] Luke 22:34
[391] Luke 7:28

If you read all the accounts of his brief ministry, you find him urging people to change their lives, seek God and do righteousness. He also wore a very uncomfortable garment and survived on a diet that most modern people would be hard pressed to even try on a bet.[392] But look at the results he attained. The people from all over the region came to him to acknowledge that their lives were not right with God and that they wanted to change. John was out in the wilderness teaching people on numerous different subjects and speaking with individuals and counselling them.

His teaching was extremely effective and when people saw him and his lifestyle, he had an authority that people respected. People recognized that here was someone who they could trust.

He had no agenda other than that of the Lord's. And what happened to him? He was killed for his beliefs. He could have recanted what he said in prison in public and been released from jail, but he believed what he had said and he was willing to bear the consequences. When the chance to deny his beliefs came, he was steadfast and suffered death because of it. Note also what John gave up. There is no mention of him having a wife and children. His life was totally devoted to the service of the Lord as his father was an ordained priest of the line of Aaron. He had a very special mission to call people to change their lives.

Now, how does this compare to raising your children? The point is, children learn by following examples, not by punishment. They also learn the same way we all do. This is by changing our own attitudes and hearts. The best lessons come by admitting we were wrong and changing our ways.

Look at the example of John the Baptist. The people round about the region that came to him learned from his example. They trusted him. They believed him. They wanted to change their ways because they saw him doing the exact things he was telling them to do. They saw him suffering for his beliefs. This is the same example we can give to our children. If don't

---

[392] See Luke 3, Matthew 2 and Mark 1

want them to lie, we should never lie and we should highlight to them how we don't lie. If we don't want them to steal, we should never steal. If you are looking for the same results that John the Baptist got, try some of his techniques. You'll find them extremely effective because they come from a divine source.

The anomalies and unfairness of life

One other aspect of Bible teaching that impacts the smacking argument concerns the contradictory lessons that smacking teaches compared to the fact that life is patently unfair. An illustration of this is helpful. Most Christians spank their children as punishment for sin they commit to train them to be better people. But does this formula always work? Not according to King Solomon, the writer of Ecclesiastes.

Life is not formula based. Something happen that can't be explained and by not preparing children for these anomalies, we do them a disservice. Job is an excellent example of this. He was a righteous man who did everything he was supposed to do, but still problems and tragedies befell him. We have to find ways to communicate these facts of life to our children to prepare them for the patent unfairness in life. Smackings don't address these facts that are outside of a formula driven existence.

In closing, I wish to refer to a quote from Dr. Randall Heskett of the Toronto School of Theology. Dr. Heskett said: "Punishment must never be equated with discipline. True discipline teaches children how to live lives that are rich and full. Training and instruction should be our aim, not punishment.[393] This training and instruction should include teaching directed to children that life has elements which can seem unfair and are not mechanically understood.

---

[393] Dr. Randall Heskett in *Interpretation Journal* April 2001 article: "Proverbs 23:13-14," pgs. 183

Appendix Three

The Biblical uses of the word "Sh'ol" and the variances in English translation found in the King James Version

It is important to provide this data to augment the argument laid out in the chapter titled: "Will a smacking save your child from going to Hell?" I provide this information to document the variations on translations offered for this single word in the Hebrew language which has led to untold confusion in applying the teaching in Proverbs 23:13-14. This data is taken from the invaluable and timeless work produced under the leadership of Mr. George Wigram titled: "The Englishman's Hebrew and Chaldee Concordance of the Old Testament." The following is taken from page 1220. The word in the various texts below that appears in *italics* is the English word that is translated from the Hebrew original "s*h'ol*."

Genesis 37:35 I will go down into the *grave*.

Genesis 42:38 my gray hairs with sorrow to the *grave*.

Genesis 44:29 my gray hairs with sorrow to the *grave*.

Genesis 44:31 gray hairs of thy servant…to the *grave*.

Numbers 16:30 they go down quick into the *pit*;

Numbers 16:33 went down alive into the *pit*,

Deuteronomy 32:22 shall burn unto the lowest *hell*,

I Samuel 2:6 he bringeth down to the *grave*,

II Samuel 22:6 The sorrows of *hell* compassed me about;

I Kings 2:6 his hoar head go down to the *grave* in peace.

I Kings 2:9 hoar head bring thou down to the *grave*

Job 7:9 he that goeth down to the *grave*

Job 11:8 deeper than *hell*; what canst thou know?

Job 14:13 wouldest hide me in the *grave*,

Job 17:13 the *grave* is mine house:

Job 17:16 They shall go down to the bars of the *pit*,

Job 21:13 in a moment go down to the *grave*.

Job 24:19 (so doth) the *grave* those which have

Job 26:9 *Hell* (is) naked before him,

Psalm 6:5 in the *grave* who shall give thee

Psalm 9:17 The wicked shall be turned into *hell*

Psalm 16:10 thou wilt not leave my soul in *hell*;

Psalm 18:5 The sorrows of *hell* compassed me

Psalm 30:3 brought up my soul from the *grave*:

Psalm 31:17 let them be silent in the *grave*.

Psalm 49:14 sheep they are laid in the *grave*;

Psalm 49:14 their beauty shall consume in the *grave*

Psalm 49:15 my soul from the power of the *grave*:

Psalm 55:15 let them go down quick into *hell*:

Psalm 86:13 delivered my soul from the lowest *hell*.

Psalm 116:3 the pains of *hell* gat hold of me:

Psalm 139:8 if I make my bed in *hell*,

Psalm 141:7 bones are scattered at the *grave's* mouth,

Proverbs 1:12 swallow them up alive as the *grave*;

Proverbs 5:5 her steps take hold on *hell*.

Proverbs 7:27 Her house (is) the way to *hell*,

Proverbs 9:18 her guests are in the depths of *hell*.

Proverbs 15:11 *Hell* and destruction (are) before the

Proverbs 15:24 depart from *hell* beneath.

Proverbs 23:14 deliver his soul from *hell*.

Proverbs 27:20 *Hell* and destruction are never full;

Proverbs 30:16 The *grave*; and the barren womb;

Ecclesiastes 9:10 no work, nor device, … in the *grave*,

Song of Songs 8:6 jealousy (is) cruel as the *grave*:

Isaiah 5:14 *hell* hath enlarged herself,

Isaiah 14:9 *Hell* (marg. or, the *grave*) from beneath is moved for thee

Isaiah 14:11 Thy pomp is brought down to the *grave*,

Isaiah 14:15 thou shalt be brought down to *hell*,

Isaiah 28:15 with *hell* are we at agreement;

Isaiah 28:18 your agreement with *hell* shall not stand;

Isaiah 38:10 I shall go to the gates of the *grave*:

Isaiah 38:18 the *grave* cannot praise thee.

Isaiah 57:9 didst debase (thyself even) unto *hell*.

Ezekiel 31:15 he went down to the *grave*

Ezekiel 31:16 I cast him down to *hell*

Ezekiel 31:17 They also went down into *hell*

Ezekiel 32:21 speak to him out of the midst of *hell*

Ezekiel 32:27 gone down to *hell* with their weapons

Hosea 13:14 ransom them from the power of the *grave*;

Hosea 13:14 O *grave*, I will be thy destruction:

Amos 9:2 Though they dig into *hell*,

Jonah 2:2 out of the belly of *hell* (marg. or, the *grave*),

Habakkuk 2:5 enlargeth his desire as *hell*,

It must be pointed out that there is no other word in the Hebrew Bible translated as "hell." Because of this, one has to ask why it was deemed necessary by the translators of the King James Version to translate this word "hell" in one place and the "grave" or "pit" in another? If you look at the texts, which feature the word "hell", it is clear that in some cases the translators themselves put the word "grave" as a marginal reference.

See Jonah 2:2 and Isaiah 14:9. The reason for this was that Jonah was obviously not in "hell" when he cried from the belly of the fish. Jonah's poetical reference here to a type of "hell" cannot be the basis for a serious doctrinal discussion

The point of this data is to show that before making pronouncements about what the Bible says about a particular subject, one should be sure that the texts from which they are speaking are clear and actually say what a person is saying they say and mean what a person says they mean. If we don't do this, we run the risk of placing ourselves in the unenviable position of having to admit that we have made a serious error. Such errors are clearly having a negative impact on the lives of young children by well-intentioned religious parents, especially those who are advocating smacking children to address issues concerning the ultimate spiritual salvation which, on the surface, seems to be the teaching in Proverbs 23:13,14.

Appendix Four

The Biblical uses of the word "Shehvet" and the variances in English translation found in the King James Version

These data are provided concerning the use of the Biblical word from the Hebrew Language that is translated as "rod." These data once again are taken from the invaluable and timeless work produced under the leadership of Mr. George Wigram titled: "The Englishman's Hebrew and Chaldee Concordance of the Old Testament." The following is taken from page 1225-6. The word in the various texts below that appears in *italics* is the English word that is translated from the Hebrew original "*Shehvet*." This word appears 181 times in the Hebrew Bible and they are listed below for any interested Bible students.

Genesis 49:10 The *sceptre* shall not depart

Genesis 49:16 as one of the *tribes* of Israel

Genesis 49:28 these are the twelve *tribes* of Israel

Exodus 21:20 if a man smite his servant ... with a *rod*

Exodus 24:4 according to the twelve *tribes* of Israel

Exodus 28:21 they be according to the twelve *tribes*.

Exodus 39:14 his name, according to the twelve *tribes*

Leviticus 27:32 whatsoever passes under the *rod*

Numbers 4:18 the *tribe* of the families of

Numbers 18:2 the *tribe* of thy father,

Numbers 24:2 abiding... according to their *tribes*;

Numbers 24:17 a *Sceptre* shall rise out of Israel,

Numbers 32:33 and unto half the *tribe* of Manasseh

Numbers 36:3 *tribes* of the children of Israel,

Deuteronomy 1:13 and known among your *tribes,*

Deuteronomy 1:15 I took the chief of your *tribes,*

Deuteronomy 1:15 officers among your *tribes.*

Deuteronomy 1:23 twelve men of you, one of a *tribe:*

Deuteronomy 3:13 I unto the half *tribe* of Manasseh;

Deuteronomy 5:23 all the heads of your *tribes,*

Deuteronomy 10:8 the Lord separated the *tribe* of Levi,

Deuteronomy 12:5 choose out of all your *tribes,*

Deuteronomy 12:14 choose in one of thy *tribes*

Deuteronomy 16:18 giveth thee, throughout thy *tribe*

Deuteronomy 18:1 (and) all the *tribe* of Levi, shall have

Deuteronomy 18:5 chosen him out of all thy *tribes*

Deuteronomy 29:8 and to the half *tribe* of Manasseh.

Deuteronomy 29:10 your captains of your *tribes,*

Deuteronomy 29:18 man, or woman, or family or *tribe,*

Deuteronomy 29:21 him unto evil out of all the *tribes* of

Deuteronomy 31:28 all the elders of your *tribes*

Deuteronomy 33:5 the *tribes* of Israel were gathered.

Joshua 1:12 and to half of the *tribe* of Manasseh , spake

Joshua 3:12 twelve men out of the *tribes* of Israel, out of every *tribe* a man

Joshua 4:2 out of every *tribe* a man,

Joshua 4:4 out of every *tribe* a man,

Joshua 4:5 the number of the *tribes* of the children

Joshua 4:8 the number of the *tribes* of the children

Joshua 4:12and half the *tribe* of Manasseh, passed

Joshua 7:14 according to your *tribes*; and it shall be (that) the *tribe* which the Lord taketh

Joshua 7:16 *tribes*; and the *tribe* of Judah was taken:

Joshua 11:23 according to their divisions by their *tribes*.

Joshua 12:6 and the half *tribe* of Manasseh.

Joshua 12:7 which Joshua gave unto the *tribes* of

Joshua 13:7 nine *tribes*, and the half tribe of Manasseh,

Joshua 13:14 unto the *tribe* of Levi he gave none

Joshua 13:29 (inheritance) unto the half *tribe* of

Joshua 13:33 But unto the *tribe* of Levi Moses gave not

Joshua 18:2 among the children of Israel seven *tribes*,

Joshua 18:4 three men for (each) *tribe*:

Joshua 18:7 and half the *tribe* of Manasseh,

Joshua 21:16 nine cities out of those two *tribes*,

Joshua 22:7 the (one) half of the *tribe* of Manasseh

Joshua 22:9 the half *tribe* of Manasseh

Joshua 22:10 the half *tribe* of Manasseh

Joshua 22:11 the half *tribe* of Manasseh

Joshua 22:13 and to the half *tribe* of Manasseh

Joshua 22:15 and to the half *tribe* of Manasseh

Joshua 22:21 the half *tribe* of Manasseh

Joshua 23:4 an inheritance for your *tribes*,

Joshua 24:1 Joshua gathered all the *tribes* of Israel

Judges 5:14 they that handle the *pen* of the writer.

Judges 18:1 the *tribe* of the Danites

Judges 18:1 fallen unto them among the *tribes* of Israel.

Judges 18:19 a priest unto a *tribe*

Judges 18:30 he and his sons were priests of the *tribe* of

Judges 20:2 (even) of all the *tribes* of Israel,

Judges 20:10 throughout all the *tribes* of Israel,

Judges 20:12 *tribes* of Israel, sent men … all the *tribes*.

Judges 21:3 one *tribe* lacking in Israel

Judges 21:5 Who (is there) among all the *tribes* of

Judges 21:6 There is one *tribe* cut off

Judges 21:8 What one (is there) of the *tribes* of Israel

Judges 21:15 had made a breach in the *tribes* of Israel.

Judges 21:17 that a *tribe* be not destroyed

Judges 21:24 every man to his *tribe*

I Samuel 2:28 I choose him out of all the *tribes* of Israel

I Samuel 9:21 of the *tribes* of Israel? And my family the least of all the families of the *tribe* of Benjamin

I Samuel 10:19 by your *tribes*, and by your thousands.

I Samuel 10:20 *tribes* of Israel to come near, the *tribe*

I Samuel 10:21 he had caused the *tribe* of Benjamin

I Samuel 15:17 (made) the head of the *tribes* of Israel,

II Samuel 5:1 Then came all the *tribes* of Israel

II Samuel 7:7 of the *tribes* (margin : judges) of Israel,

II Samuel 7:14 I will chasten him with the *rod* of men,

II Samuel 15:2 servant (is) of one of the *tribes* of Israel,

II Samuel 15:10 spies throughout all the *tribes* of Israel,

II Samuel 18:14 he took three *darts* in his hand,

II Samuel 19:9 strife throughout all the *tribes* of Israel,

II Samuel 20:14 he went through all the *tribes* of Israel.

II Samuel 23:21 no city out of all the *tribes* of Israel

II Samuel 24:2 Go now through all the *tribes* of Israel

I Kings 8:16 chose no city out of all the *tribes* of Israel

I Kings 11:13 will give one *tribe* to thy son:

I Kings 11:31 and will give ten *tribes* to thee:

I Kings 11:32 But he shall have one *tribe*

I Kings 11:32 chosen out of all the *tribes* of Israel:

I Kings 11:35 will give it unto thee, (even) ten *tribes*.

I Kings 11:36 unto his son will I give one *tribe*,

I Kings 12:20 but the *tribe* of Judah only.

I Kings 12:21 house of Judah, with the *tribe* of Benjamin

I Kings 14:21 did choose out of all the *tribes* of Israel

I Kings 18:31 the *tribes* of the sons of Jacob,

II Kings 17:18 there was none left but the *tribe* of Judah

II Kings 21:7 I have chosen out of all the *tribes* of Israel

I Chronicles 5:18 and half the *tribe* of Manasseh

I Chronicles 5:23 children of the half *tribe* of Manasseh

I Chronicles 5:26 and the half *tribe* of Manasseh

I Chronicles 11:23 went down to him with a *staff*

I Chronicles 12:37 and of the half *tribe* of Manasseh

I Chronicles 23:14 sons were named of the *tribe* of Levi

I Chronicles 26:32 and the half *tribe* of Manasseh

I Chronicles 27:16 Furthermore over the *tribes* of Israel

I Chronicles 27:20 of the half *tribe* of Manasseh, Joel

I Chronicles 27:22 the princes of the *tribes* of Israel.

I Chronicles 28:1 the princes of the *tribes*,

I Chronicles 29:6 and princes of the *tribes* of Israel.

II Chronicles 6:5 no city among all the *tribes* of Israel

II Chronicles 11:16 out of all the *tribes* of Israel such

II Chronicles 12:13 chosen out of all the *tribes* of Israel,

II Chronicles 33:7 chosen before all the *tribes* of Israel,

Job 9:34 Let him take his *rod* away

Job 21:9 neither (is) the *rod* of God upon them.

Job 37:13 for *correction* (marg. a *rod*), or for his land,

Psalm 2:9 Thou shalt break them with a *rod* of iron;

Psalm 23:4 thy *rod* and thy staff they comfort me:

Psalm 45:6 *sceptre* of thy kingdom (is) a right *sceptre*.

Psalm 74:2 the *rod* (marg. or, *tribe*) of thine

Psalm 78:55 made the *tribes* of Israel to dwell

Psalm 78:67 and chose not the *tribe* of Ephraim:

Psalm 78:68 But chose the *tribe* of Judah,

Psalm 89:32 will I visit their transgressions with the *rod*,

Psalm 105:37 not one feeble (person) among their *tribes*,

Psalm 122:4 Whither the *tribes* go up, the *tribes* of the

Psalm 125:3 the *rod* of the wicked shall not rest

Proverbs 10:13 but a *rod* (is) for the back of him that

Proverbs 13:24 He that spareth his *rod* hateth his son:

Proverbs 22:8 and the *rod* of his anger shall fail.

Proverbs 23:13 beatest him with the *rod*,

Proverbs 23:14 Thou shalt beat him with the *rod*,

Proverbs 26:3 and a *rod* for the fool's back.

Proverbs 29:15 The *rod* and reproof give wisdom:

Isaiah 9:4 the *rod* of his oppressor, as in the day

Isaiah 10:5 O Assyrian, the *rod* of mine anger,

Isaiah 10:15 as if the *rod* should shake (itself)

Isaiah 10:24 he shall smite thee with a *rod*,

Isaiah 11:4 he shall smite the earth with a *rod* of

Isaiah 14:5 the *sceptre* of the rulers.

Isaiah 14:29 the *rod* of him that smote thee

Isaiah 19:13 the stay of the *tribes*

Isaiah 28:27 the cumin with a *rod*,

Isaiah 30:31 the Assyrian…(which) smote with a *rod*.

Isaiah 49:6 to raise up the *tribes* of Jacob,

Isaiah 63:17 the *tribes* of thine inheritance:

Jeremiah 10:16 Israel (is) the *rod* of his inheritance:

Jeremiah 51:19 and (Israel is) the *rod* of his inheritance:

Lamentations 3:1 seen affliction by the *rod* of his wrath.

Ezekiel 19:11 the *sceptres* of them that bare rule,

Ezekiel 19:14 no strong *rod* (to be) a *sceptre* to rule.

Ezekiel 20:37 I will cause you to pass under the *rod*,

Ezekiel 21:10 the *rod* of my son,

Ezekiel 21:13 if (the sword) contemn even the *rod*?

Ezekiel 37:19 and the *tribes* of Israel his fellows,

Ezekiel 45:8 of Israel according to their *tribes*.

Ezekiel 47:13 according to the twelve *tribes* of Israel:

Ezekiel 47:21 unto you according to the *tribes* of Israel.

Ezekiel 47:22 among the *tribes* of Israel.

Ezekiel 47:23 in what *tribe* the stranger sojourneth,

Ezekiel 48:1 the names of the *tribes*.

Ezekiel 48:19 serve it out of all the *tribes* of Israel.

Ezekiel 48:23 the rest of the *tribes*,

Ezekiel 48:29 divide by lot unto the *tribes* of Israel

Ezekiel 48:31 after the names of the *tribes* of Israel:

Hosea 5:9 among the *tribes* of Israel have I made

Amos 1:5 him that holdeth the *sceptre*

Amos 1:8 him that holdeth the *sceptre*

Micah 5:1 they shall smite the judge of Israel with a *rod*

Micah 7:14 Feed thy people with thy *rod*,

Zechariah 9:1 as of all the *tribes* of Israel,

Zechariah 10:11 and the *sceptre* of Egypt shall depart

Appendix Five

The order of the Hebrew Bible books
versus the order found in Protestant Bible versions

As mentioned in chapter four, the order of the books of the Hebrew Bible is different than that of the modern Protestant Bible versions. Let us be clear and exact when we understand without any ambiguity, that only the order is different. We are not talking about different or fewer or more books, we are only speaking about the arrangement of the books and how they were organized in ancient times (the order of which has been preserved today in Hebrew Bible versions).

This information is referred to exactly by Jesus in Luke 24:44,45 when he mentioned the reference to "the Law, the Prophets and the Psalms." Let us look at this order. It is most instructive because it represents the divinely inspired order transmitted from antiquity.

The Law

Protestant Bible Version Order	Hebrew Bible Order
Genesis	Genesis
Exodus	Exodus
Leviticus	Leviticus
Numbers	Numbers
Deuteronomy	Deuteronomy

The Prophets

Protestant Bible Version Order	Hebrew Bible Order
Joshua	Joshua/Judges
Judges	I & II Samuel & I & II Kings
I Samuel	Isaiah
II Samuel	Jeremiah
I Kings	Ezekiel
II Kings	The Twelve Minor Prophets
I Chronicles	(From Hosea to Malachi as in
II Chronicles	Protestant Bible Versions)
Ezra	
Nehemiah	
Esther	
Job	
Psalms	
Proverbs	
Ecclesiastes	
Song of Songs	

Note: In the original Hebrew versions of the Bible, the books Joshua and Judges were originally reckoned as only one book as were the books I & II Samuel and I & II Kings. The same is the case for twelve Minor prophets from Hosea to Malachi.

The Psalms - (or Holy Writings as they are also called)

Protestant Bible Version Order	Hebrew Bible Order
Isaiah	Psalms
Jeremiah	Proverbs
Lamentations	Job
Ezekiel	Song of Songs
Daniel	Ruth
Hosea	Lamentations
Joel	Ecclesiastes
Amos	Esther
Obadiah	Daniel
Jonah	Ezra/Nehemiah
Micah	I & II Chronicles
Nahum	
Habakkuk	
Zephaniah	
Haggai	
Zechariah	
Malachi	

Note: In the original Hebrew versions of the Bible, the books of Ezra and Nehemiah were originally reckoned as only one book as were I & II Chronicles.

In the original order of the books and the proper divisions spoken of by Christ in Luke 24:24,45 and maintained by Hebrew versions today, the information provided in chapter four comes through when one takes into consideration the inspired order of the Hebrew Bible. This interpretation cannot make sense utilizing the Protestant Bible versions and the chronological order adopted over the last 1,600 years.

Appendix Six

St. Augustine on corporal punishment

St. Augustine (354-430) was born in North Africa of a Christian mother and he is recognized as one of the great scholars of the Christian faith. He has some very interesting comments to make concerning early childhood, including expressing his view on corporal punishment.

According to Professor Martha Ellen Stortz, Augustine was a highly sensitive and careful student of children in all phases of life. Augustine's classification of the stages of life is similar to that outlined by Edersheim referenced earlier in this book.[394] He saw six phases of human life of which infancy was the first. Infancy was from birth to the time where language was acquired. "Augustine watched infants closely and attempted to put into words this world without language."[395]

"Augustine described tenderly the smiles of sleep and the comfort of nursing, but juxtaposed these occasions of serenity with a newborn's jealous rage when, even after it had been fed, it saw another infant a a nurse's breast."[396]

While children in this age of life can exhibit temper tantrums and extreme acts which many modern Christian smacking advocates have urged parents to repress with corporal punishment, Augustine gave no such advice.

---

[394] See pages 15-32
[395] Stortz, The Child in Christian Thought, art. *"Where or When Was Your Servant Innocent?"*, pg. 83
[396] Stortz, The Child in Christian Thought, art. *"Where or When Was Your Servant Innocent?"*, pg. 84

On the contrary, he "judged the tantrum that followed unworthy of punishment: without language the infant could not understand the rebuke."[397] To Augustine, "Language introduced the difference between obedience and disobedience, for which a child was accountable."[398]

Stortz then goes on to show Augustine's attitude toward corporal punishment that "despite this increasing accountability, Augustine could not condone the many beatings he had received as a child. He archly observed that both adults and children played games, yet children were the ones who got punished for playing them! That basic inequity between children and adults marked his childhood: 'The schoolmaster who caned me was behaving no better than I was.' Though childhood was full of reprehensible actions, Augustine did not favour punishing children as severely as adults. Hopefully with maturity 'reason begins to take hold,' and rationale behind the rules becomes clearer, making willing obedience a possibility."[399]

It is important to note, Augustine does not appeal to the book of Proverbs and the texts advocating smacking children. His line of thinking is remarkably similar to that advocated by early Jewish scholars showing that young children should never be smacked because "young children simply couldn't understand intellectually why they are being punished and what punishment is meant to do for them."[400]

---

[397] ibid., Stortz here quotes Colin Starnes, Augustine's Conversion: A Guide to the Argument of Confessions I-IX (Waterloo, Ont.: Wilfrid Laurier Univ. Press 1990), p. 10
[398] ibid.
[399] ibid.
[400] See page 44 of this volume

About the Author

Samuel Martin was born in England and is the youngest child of Dr. Ernest L. and Helen R. Martin, who are both Americans. He lived in the UK for the first seven years of his life before moving to the USA with his family. He lived in the USA until 2001 when he married a native Israeli and relocated to live in Jerusalem.

He and his wife, Sonia, have two daughters.

His experience with biblical scholarship began at an early age. His father lead a program in conjunction with Hebrew University and the late Professor Benjamin Mazar, where over a five year period, some 450 college students came to work on an archaeological excavation in Jerusalem starting in 1969.

Since that first trip, Samuel has visited Israel on 14 different occasions living more than 19 years of his life in the country. He has toured all areas of Israel as well as worked in several archaeological excavations.

He writes regularly on biblical subjects with a particular interest in children, families, nature, science, the Bible, and gender in the Biblical context.

Website: www.biblechild.com
Contact: info@biblechild.com
Facebook: https://www.facebook.com/byblechyld/
Blog: www.samuelmartin.blogspot.com

REVIEWS

"I've had a chance to read through your manuscript and I find it very interesting! I think you've made an important contribution, especially to contextualizing biblical ideas about childrearing. I hope you will find a publisher for this book. I'm sure many others would benefit from learning of your research."

Dr. Dawn Devries
Professor of Systematic Theology
Union Theological Seminary
Contributor to the book, *"The Child in Christian Thought"* (Eerdmans: 2000)

"Thank you very much for your manuscript ... I found some of your passages very, very interesting,... It would be of great interest to parents..."

Fr. Lawrence Boadt
CSP, Publisher, Paulist Press

"Many thanks for sending me a copy of your book. Since I, like so many, cannot read Hebrew, I found your analysis of language fascinating and persuasive. Your exploration of these complex issues is thorough and convincing."

Dr. Philip Greven,
Professor Emeritus, Rutgers University,
Author of *"Spare the Child: The Religious Roots of Punishment and the Psychological Impact of Physical Abuse"* (Random House, 1992)

"This is not an easy read, but it is one any Christian who desires to be true to the Bible in the first instance should take time to read....In my view this study is a definitive reading of the biblical texts for Christians and non-Christians alike."

Rev. Alistair McBride,
Scots Presbyterian Church, Hamilton, New Zealand
(see www.repeal59.blogspot.com - July 25 2006)

"I want to take my hat off to Samuel Martin and say, Thanks! When I think about Samuel Martin, what comes to mind is a contemporary and contextualized, this-world version of William Wilberforce. He certainly has Wilberforce blood running through his veins. He is a Christian living in Jerusalem with an interest in connecting to the rest of the world in ways that are helpful and strategic about how to live out ones faith. Check his website: http://samuelmartin.blogspot.com/. You will find interesting discussions about various biblical subjects.

In addition to being a blogger, Samuel is an author. I just finished reading his book *Thy Rod and Thy Staff They Comfort Me: Christians and the Spanking Controversy*...

Unlike more academic books that I tend to write, which can often be inaccessible to average readers (!), Samuel Martin does a good job of writing with an easy-to-understand touch. For me the greatest benefit in reading his book was to see how a movement towards an anti-spanking position can be developed through Jewish sources and readings of Scripture (as well as Christian ones). He comes to similar conclusions that I do regarding the spanking controversy but his path through the biblical material is quite different, fascinating read.

Blogger, author and, most importantly, activist! My third thanks to Samuel is that he has reminded me of my own need to be at least to some extent . . . an activist. He has not done this by way of harassment. No, he has shown me this through his own life and example. He would be happy to know that recently I have broken out of my insulated scholarly circles and actually done a handful of radio interviews. Now that is a stretch for a stuffy, old professor of New Testament. Through his own activist work, quite extensive as I have watched from afar, he is changing the world one person at a time. He does so often by putting people together in ways that help to bring influence on those who perhaps would otherwise not listen. Samuel has reminded me of something that is easily forgotten in the ivory towers of academia, namely, that ideas only work to the degree that there are people willing to influence (other) people about those ideas. So, on three accounts my hat is off to Samuel Martin, blogger, author and activist."

Professor William Webb
Adjunct Professor of Biblical Studies
In addition to conference speaking ministry, he has published several articles and books, including *Returning Home* (Sheffield Press, 1993), *Slaves, Women, and Homosexuals* (InterVarsity, 2001), *Discovering Biblical Equality* (two chapters; InterVarsity, 2005), *Four Views on Moving from the Bible to Theology* (one view and responses; Zondervan, 2009), *Corporal Punishment in the Bible: A Redemptive Hermeneutic for Troubling Texts* (InterVarsity, 2011).

"A thoughtful and fulsome refutation of widely-held ideas that perpetuate violence against children. A very important intellectual contribution to an often-emotional debate."

Professor Joan Durrant
Professor of Community Health Sciences
University of Manitoba

"Wonderful resource both for advocates/researchers who want to counter "the Bible tells me so" argument about spanking."

Professor Elizabeth Gershoff
Professor of Human Development and Family Sciences
University of Texas at Austin

"I am pleased to endorse Samuel Martin's book *Thy Rod and they Staff They Comfort Me: Christians and the Smacking Controversy*. The book provides a very readable, thoughtful, balanced, scholarly, and thorough analysis of the Biblical basis of corporal punishment of children. I have frequently recommended it to others who seek to learn more about Biblical references to smacking. In fact, it is a must-read for anyone who wants to become more informed about the topic."

Professor George Holden
Professor of Psychology
Southern Methodist University
He is a noted expert on parenting, discipline and family violence.

"Your work on kids, ... , occupies a critical position on the frontlines in the fight against brutality in Christianity. Kids don't need to have their sinful nature beaten out of them."

Professor Curtis Hutt
Judaic Studies
University of Nebraska at Omaha.

"These and other verses, as well as the overall teaching about disciplining children in the Bible is ably discussed by Jerusalem-based Christian biblical scholar Samuel Martin, who has produced a wonderful book, *Thy Rod and Thy Staff They Comfort Me: Christians and the Spanking Controversy*,... Martin has been joined by a significant number of other informed Christian scholars and commentators who are questioning the both the traditional translation and interpretation of these overly quoted verses from the book of Proverbs, see for example, *Christians Have No Moral Rationale for Spanking Children*. I recommend Martin's work for those biblically oriented folk out there who have wondered about what the Bible really says regarding using corporeal punishment of any kind to discipline children—or for that matter anyone who wants to be more informed on this controversial topic."

James D. Tabor
Professor of ancient Judaism and early Christianity
Chair (2004-2014) of the Department of Religious Studies
University of North Carolina
Previously he held positions at the University of Notre Dame and the College of William and Mary. He received his Ph.D. from the University of Chicago in 1981 in Ancient Mediterranean Religions.

Made in the
USA
Middletown, DE